An American Militiaman's Handbook

By John M. Leyzorek

AF409275

FOREWORD to the First (2021) Edition

As the founder of AmericaAgain! Trust and its action mission TACTICAL CIVICS™, when I met West Virginian John Leyzorek in November 2017, I had no idea that in just three years he would hammer out the next level of application for 40 years of work by my Militia mentors, Edwin Vieira of Virginia and Jon Roland of Texas.

John is developing the most exciting and logical approach to restoring constitutional Militias of these sovereign States, at the county level. John doesn't merely write treatises and join me on Sunday nights to tape our TACTICAL CIVICS™ LibertyCasts. For years, he has also worked on the ground with private 'militia' groups around the country.

Militiamen are familiar with the *Posse Comitatus Act* of 1878, which stipulates that federal military cannot operate within any State. In early Rome, the government's armed forces did many things. They waged wars of invasion, plunder, and occupation. They waged supposedly 'defensive' wars to keep control of states that it was occupying. They put pressure on subjugated peoples to pay tribute and taxes. And they also kept the peace in all of Rome's towns, whether in captured lands or in Italy; and like modern police, also in the city of Rome itself.

Like the Caesars, Washington DC over the past 130 years has invaded almost every sovereign country on earth in our name. But first it had to subdue the sovereign States of America! During Lincoln's overthrow of our Constitution, after destroying half of all property in America, Washington DC's 12-year military occupation, called *Reconstruction,* was the accurate label for its capture, occupation, and reprogramming of every state; exactly ancient Rome's practice with its captive states. This is why we always use the historically correct term for Lincoln's war: *The War to Enslave the States.*

In early England from the end of the ninth century AD, *posse comitatus* roughly meant, 'the power of the county', and the *shire reeve* was the strong arm of the crown, collecting taxes and calling up *housecarls* to quell riots when the people became discontented.

Sheriffs arrested and punished the worst criminals…but not the *crown's* criminals or ruthless, lawless aristocracy who paid the crown's expenses. The oligarchs did whatever they liked, as Clintons, Comeys, Obamas, Bidens, governors, mayors and others do in our lawless Republic today. So you see that sheriffs have an ancient history as law enforcement; but enforcing the *king's* laws, not the Common Law born in the Compact of Æthelred in 1014 AD and reinforced by Magna Carta in 1215 AD.

This is why our Founding Fathers were against career military and 'law enforcement', and why sheriffs have not helped restore constitutional militias. On the other side, it's equally difficult to convince passionate American men who want to be militia, to follow the constitutional process to make their groups legitimate.

Thus, the same two opposing forces still exist: the crown's shire reeve against the people's massed forces who form mobs when tyrants become unbearable, as happened with our War of Independence.

Of all the elements of wisdom in our Constitution, the most vital to civilization are our two ancient law enforcement institutions, Grand Jury and Militia. *Both must be performed by the People, without pay.* For five generations, government schools have erased our true history and study of our unique, powerful Constitution, but by God's grace: 1) It is still the 'supreme Law of the Land'; 2) Every public servant is sworn to uphold it; and 3) Militia is its *only* lawful enforcement.

As in ancient Rome and Great Britain, career armies, police, and sheriffs forces have displaced Militia. *Our Founding Fathers were stridently against this.*

Now comes TACTICAL CIVICS™, a responsible new way of life for the repentant Remnant to restore both institutions *together in each county,* and for the Militia half, this book is the first to offer a clear, detailed plan to do it.

David M. Zuniga
New Bag End, Boerne, Texas

Table of Contents

SECTION I
Introduction

CHAPTER 1
History

Probably equal numbers of Americans today love and revere, hate and fear, and have never heard of, "Militia".

The word "Militia" comes from the Latin, *miles* meaning "soldier", but it does not mean a regular, paid soldier, or a standing army under the command of a national leadership. Militia has always meant ALL the people of a community, traditionally its men of fighting age, trained, possessing their own arms, and ready to defend it.

In its most fundamental and ancient legal sense, it is merely the collective expression of the inherent and unalienable right of armed self-defense. In our English common-law heritage, it was the counter-balance to the dictatorial rule of arrogant kings, as well as the "homeland security" of every village, not only described but mandated by law, well before the 10th century A.D.

We find it as a ubiquitous and conspicuous feature of the American colonies, where it develops its unique American character. It carries this into its crucial places in our Constitution, in Article I Section 8, Clauses 15 and 16, and, of course, in the Second Amendment. The former, while describing Congress' duties, enumerate Militia's Constitutional functions:

15 To provide for calling forth the <u>Militia to execute the Laws of the Union, suppress Insurrections and repel Invasions</u>; (emphasis added)

16 To provide for organizing, arming, and disciplining, the Militia, and for governing such Part of them as may be employed in the Service of the United States, reserving to the States respectively, the Appointment of the Officers, and the Authority of training the Militia according to the discipline prescribed by Congress;

'Execute the Laws' is a duty of Militia unique to America, and reflects two uniquely American realities. First, it should be the core of our modern security, protecting us from the evil in our own natures and from its expression by our servants in government. Second, We The People in America made our own law, for our own protection, and We The People hold the ultimate and highest authority to interpret, apply, and enforce it[1]. Not the cop on the beat. Not the sheriff. Not the DA, governor, congress, or any of the alphabet agencies. Not even the U.S. Supreme Court

And if the origin of our law is not enough, lest it be thought that these powers are conferred by or emanate from Congress, observe that the text does *not* say, "provide for *authorizing,* or *empowering"*. The authorities of Militia recognized here were clearly thought to be inherent.

1

  "The U.S. supreme Court is not the highest authority in the land on constitutional law. We are." Former Stanford Law School dean Larry Kramer, *The People Themselves: Popular Constitutionalism and Judicial Review,* pg. 248

CHAPTER 2

Militia Today

But where, and what, is Militia in America today? For over a century, neither Congress nor any State has performed its constitutional duty to support it. The Constitution, our highest human Law, is barely a memory in the halls of government. Insurrection is boiling in many of our cities, and the ongoing illegal alien invasion left the front pages only when shoved aside to make room for the COVID psyop and a parade of anti-Trump trumpery.

Law schools and states' attorneys are distributing articles claiming that militia-type training and activity is positively against the law. And the media represent militia as dangerous gangs of ignorant, racist, anti-government vigilantes.

At the same time, actual citizens' groups often calling themselves 'militias' are multiplying across the country. Most of them do train to fight, but spend most of their energy assisting the elderly, running food banks, teaching and working on disaster preparedness, cleanup and recovery, and a variety of other community services. Most have excellent reputations in their own communities, and many partner with their local sheriffs and other paid law enforcement agencies.

Militia is also the *only* thing described as 'necessary' in our Constitution. This means that any supposed 'law' that interferes with it is repugnant to the Constitution, therefore void[2]. Militia is the

---

2

heart of the lawful, practical solution to most of the troubles that are eroding our freedom, destroying our communities, and tearing our country apart.

"All laws which are repugnant to the Constitution are null and void."
(Marbury vs. Madison , 1803.)

CHAPTER 3
Purpose of This Book

This book is designed to help communities form and operate constitutional Militia, and to help existing armed groups enhance their capabilities for the purposes enumerated in our Constitution. To fulfill these purposes, it *must* be coordinated with that other component of community organization, the government. The window of opportunity to do this today lies at the county or city level.

Before you throw this book across the room in anger: we agree that most portions of 'our' government today do not feel like 'ours' at all. But we can't dismiss or ignore them, nor should we hate or fear or reject them, any more than we junk a good car when the gas tank is empty, the tires are worn out, somebody has crossed wires, or we make a wrong turn in it and get lost. It helps to know the fundamental design of our system of government, of which we are the top level. That is reflected by the opening sentence of our Constitution, which begins, "We, the People...do ordain..."

As you see, for any American to say or think, "I'm against the government" would be a mistake. We The People created a Constitution by which we created our servant government, but kept ourselves as the highest level of it! I mentioned above that the Militia function in America is unique on earth, but so is our entire system of government.

So. The chores fall to us, the collective sovereign. Like it or not. The process of coordinating our Militia with the rest of our government is the most powerful, practical first step to *repair* it, bringing government at all levels back to its lawful functions as *our servant*. This book shows you how.

Timing

At this writing (early 2023) we are at a crossroads. For decades, government at all levels, and the system of law that we allowed it to monopolize and corrupt, have been losing our respect while taking over more and more of our lives. The 9/11 debacle in Manhattan, DC, and Shanksville, PA was not the first deliberate, murderous false-flag atrocity perpetrated by our criminal servants in government. But it woke up a substantial number of patriotic Americans to what our servants had become, and was a marked escalation in participation of many agencies of our government in a global campaign for totalitarian world government.

Obama was our first overtly anti-American president. The globalists pulled out all the stops to get rid of our answer, the Americanist Trump. In doing so, the evil cabal destroyed what most of us regarded as our ultimate means to control government: elections. Until We the People take back our responsibilities, we will never again be able to vote our way out of this. Incidentally, Obama's cabal is still very much in control of the DC apparatus; a subject for another day.

We must finally come to terms with the hard fact that we can no longer trust our institutions to defend our freedom, laws, or culture. As our Founders understood, we must do it *ourselves*. That means we must restore Militia, and we must get it right.

SECTION II
Purposes of Militia

Our inspired Constitution is not the Bible; it does not speak to us as individuals or communities. The Ninth Amendment reads, *"The enumeration in the Constitution, of certain rights, shall not be construed to deny or disparage others retained by the people."* Its purpose is to narrowly define the *structure*, and exhaustively and exclusively enumerate (limit) the *powers*, of our federal servant, and how We the People are to enforce those limitations.

Thus, our Constitution charges Militia with certain tasks. But its place in its community is wider than those three charges in Clause 15. Militia is a pre-constitutional entity, as old as the need to band together to chase away the wolves or defend against the barbarians from the next valley.

It's Not About "My Guns!"

To identify with its community, its membership must include all who are willing and qualified, and it must respond to community needs beyond those three Constitutional charges. So, while Militia must train and prepare to apply force-on-force for its explicit constitutional duties, it must invest equal energy in community service, preparation, and protection. Such activities that many Militias engage in include:

- Food and clothing distribution to the needy

- Adopt-a-highway or other community cleanup projects

- Firewood-to-the-widow, rides to the hospital, leaky-roof repair, or other targeted aid to individuals with a special need

- Classes in firearms safety and church/home/business security

- Safety and security services for churches, businesses, festivals, accidents, severe weather events

- Search-and rescue services

- Gardening and food-preservation classes; assistance with garden preparation (e.g. plowing or tilling)

- Blood drives

Activities like these are not Militia jobs, in the legal or historical sense. But they are not optional for any modern American Militia. First, it is simply a moral obligation for all of us to assist our neighbor. Secondly, humanitarian activities by the members of your Militia also build familiarity, dispel fear, and earn the confidence of your community. Without the confidence of your community, you will not have its support in donations, flow of essential information, recruitment, safe harbor under hostile circumstances, cooperation with its preparedness advice, and support when you seek local government's recognition. This is the essence of government of, by, and for the People.

Constitutional Law Enforcement

The most unfamiliar yet most urgent function of Militia in peacetime is Law Enforcement. As we put it in the Constitution, *"...Militia, to execute the Laws of the Union"*.

Notice that in the Constitution, we do not create, authorize, or even *mention* sheriff, state police, or municipal police. Yet Militia need not and must not try to 'defund' or replace them. In fact, every Militia should work to establish friendly, mutually supportive relationships with them, *as long as they are abiding by the Law.* However, none of these agencies has constitutional authority, as Militia does.

Paid law-enforcement, such as the sheriff's department, and the city and state police, are always limited in numbers and thus in effectiveness by the cost to the taxpayers of their salaries. Worse, they are often political, and integral parts of the government apparatus. This makes them susceptible to pressures to lean hard on some and go light on others. They depend for their salaries and job tenure on politicians. Not many will go against the boss or the paymaster, however bad he may be.

Moreover, as paid careerists in the institutional government, they all are concerned for their paychecks, budgets, retirement plans, and suffer from every bureaucratic disease. They are unwilling or unable to arrest or even investigate official corruption, for they cannot bite the hand that feeds them. Budget limitations, and sometimes plain corruption, also often prevent them from confronting powerful private criminal operations within the county.

This has been true since ancient times, of course.

Militia, on the other hand, is volunteers. Even if the local government chooses to support them with training ammo or meeting space, Militia provides huge law-enforcement manpower at minimal cost. Although Constitutional Militia is necessarily integrated with government by government's recognition and by Militia's cooperation with the court system, Militia is We, the People ourselves, subordinate to no official, and responsible only to our neighbors, to the Constitution and laws made in pursuance thereof, , and to God.

For these reasons, the Militia must act as the point of the spear to restore our society. We have a Constitution, and every public servant takes an oath to obey it. It is our highest law! Therefore, our government servants' invasions on our rights and attacks on our culture and livelihoods are not tyranny in the ancient sense; they are merely organized crime: concerted actions by our paid servants that are instantly recognized as assault, robbery, unlawful imprisonment, fraud, deprivation of rights under color of law, and many other common crimes, when private citizens commit them.

The Other Equal Partner

Militia can srop crime in progress, like any citizen, and provides force if necessary, but it does not investigate. That task today largely belongs to paid police and State, County or City attorneys or prosecutors, not to mention the unconstitutional FBI.

This puts discovery of crime in inherently unreliable hands. These bodies all are political, all want to look good by collaring lots of.....sometimes....bad-guys, sometimes political enemies, and sometimes poor Joe who just was in the wrong place at the wrong time, or got pulled in to make a bureaucratic quota. And none of these agencies will take on the big criminals: the crooked DA or judge or city manager, or big-time drug-dealer, or legislator himself, who runs the show and controls the money and the votes, and has what amounts to a private army of security and propaganda staffers

So, Militia needs a partner in this task, because perhaps the most important feature of our legal system is *due process*. Everyone's rights must be respected, and every official act must have a transparent reason.

Militia's law-enforcement partner, proven in centuries of Common Law and incorporated in our system by our Constitution, is the Grand Jury. It is seated usually by a judge, but is drawn at random from We, the People, just like the more familiar petit jury. It is the other People's institution that is much older than the Constitution, but also acknowledged and required in that law.

With roots over a thousand years old, Grand Jury is not supposed to be the rubber stamp of prosecutors and judges. As U.S. supreme court justice Antonin Scalia explained in the 1992 case *U.S. v Williams* , the Grand Jury is We The People ourselves, empaneled by a court or sheriff but completely outside their control, by design. The Grand Jury has the authority to investigate any wrongdoing in its jurisdiction; to examine records, summon witnesses by subpoena, issue search and arrest warrants for evidence or suspects, and hand down felony indictments.

Drawing on the People's intimate knowledge of their own

community, and with its total independence of and superior authority to servant government, the Grand Jury is the American People's ideal, natural process to uncover official lawlessness and corruption even in judges, prosecutors, sheriffs, and legislators.

Embodying the power of Law and Truth, it's the perfect and necessary partner to the armed power of Militia. A Grand Jury, even if it knows its full power and duty, cannot reach official corruption or organized crime if it only has the often political, career-protecting paid police agencies to execute its warrants. And Militia, however well trained and armed, cannot *lawfully* stop crime or bring criminals to trial, without evidence and formal charge.

We The People, Making History (again)

This must be the first act of the larger plan called TACTICAL CIVICS™, developed by the organization of the same name. It is the first solution in history, that includes discrete action plans and documentation to brief and restore the two ancient, pre-constitutional law enforcement institutions, *and have them coordinate and support one another in each county.*

The historic range of crimes against our civilization have finally driven We The People to turn to God in repentance. Through years of diligent research, discussion, and soul-searching, the team at TACTICAL CIVICS™, on which I proudly served from 2017 to 2022, developed this historic yet common sense restoration project for our unique and precious American rule of law.

To fill its desperately needed role in our communities, Militia must earn the same level of regard that we have for volunteer fire companies: the guys we can count on when we're in trouble, and also the guys that we want to be like.

SECTION III
Functions & Structure of a Militia

Form follows function.
The body needs to move, so it has legs.
It needs to avoid bumping into things, so it has eyes.
It needs to decide what to do, so it has a brain.
So also with a Militia.

CHAPTER 1
Membership

First and foremost, a Militia is people. So it has membership functions. You need a Membership Officer or Committee, whose duties include recruiting and vetting new members, keeping track of needs and special skills of individual members, maintaining membership lists (date of admission and oath, contact information, availability, and level of health, skills and training, and level of trust of each member), and maintaining the security of such lists. In theory, Militia should be 'the whole people'; in practice, to support safety and effectiveness we need to establish qualifications.

General Qualifications

Membership should be open to any citizen or legal resident of the State or of the United States, residing in or having ties to the county or other political subdivision where the Militia is to operate.

Paid officials or employees of any level of government, with executive or supervisory responsibility, must be excluded. Their loyalty will be divided between their interests on the one hand as individuals, families, and members of the community, and on the other hand as members of the power structure, or employees with a boss who is a politician with power or 'turf' of his own, and a paycheck to protect. We're not suggesting that all paid officials with executive or supervisory roles are bad people. But they're human.

Non-supervisory public employees like water plant or garbage truck workers or highway maintenance workers, even though they need their paychecks, are often very knowledgeable about local infrastructure and the foibles of the bureaucracy, and they are already contributing great effort to the welfare of the community. They can be assets to the Militia.

Convicted Felons

A significant number of people get convicted in error. Good arguments may be made that many harmless actions are today wrongfully defined as felonies. But in general, persons who have been convicted of a felony in any State should not be admitted to full membership. Reasons for this include felony-related restrictions on firearms possession, the need for public trust in the Militia, the need for the support of local government, and the bare fact that many who used very bad judgement once are more likely than most to do it again.

Of course, individuals who were wrongly convicted, or are honestly reformed and want to seek the position of highest trust and usefulness in the community as Militia members, should be encouraged to pursue legal processes to reverse or expunge their convictions.

Oaths and Allegiances

It is customary for Militia members to swear an oath, as a minimum to uphold the Constitution of the State and of the United States. For a sample, see Appendix G.

Unfortunately, there are certain other groups that should as a rule be excluded from service in Militia. Followers of Mohammed are encouraged by their 'holy book' to lie if necessary to promote the eventual dominance of Islam over all people. They are taught that they have a right to the persons and property of all non-Moslems, and that they are at war against all non-Moslem countries. Beliefs and loyalties of this type are anti-American, anti-constitutional, dangerous to the community, make the believer untrustworthy, and render any oath a believer may take, non-credible.

Individually, most Moslems are surely trying to be good people. But unless you have overwhelming evidence of their devotion to truth, God's Law, our Constitution and to their whole community, it is not advisable to entrust to them the safety of all.

Skills Assessment

Militia needs every skill available in the community, so all ages and levels of ability should be welcomed. Even a unit narrowly directed at fighting needs cooks, bandage rollers, message runners, people to sit and monitor radio traffic, people who gather gossip, medics and nurses, vehicle drivers, mechanics, electronics and computer techs, and carpenters. Your group even needs PR; people who can make it look good by describing its activities in favorable but honest terms.

Speaking of public relations, although official violence is condoned in Romans 13, human nature guarantees that some individuals will seek Militia duty, as some seek employment in law-enforcement, at least partly to gratify unhealthy appetites. Any enlisted man can tell you of officers who daily illustrated this sin, and you may have met a 'law enforcement officer' or two who displayed it. Gangs use this sin as their necessary currency to keep members intimidated.

Background Checks

Vetting means checking out a possible member to prevent trouble later, from individuals with bad morals, judgement, principles or self-control. There are many ways to do it; but it's an imperfect process, and a craft that takes time to master. Whatever process you design, *apply it uniformly.* Don't take a shortcut because the candidate is your brother-in-law or the sheriff's nephew. Nothing can destroy the morale and trust in Militia units more quickly than favoritism or nepotism.

Social media are easy to check and they often reveal a great deal. Your application should ask for names and Internet places where the applicant posts. Look for wild, stupid, nasty, immoral, violent, or lawless posts. Be on the lookout for 'likes' of inappropriate things. You should ask for employer and personal references, and credit checks are available from many sources. Poor credit history often correlates with irresponsibility.

Criminal background checks are available (for a fee) from many online sources and through the state police or other official agencies in many states. Before you decide that this process is too expensive or intrusive for your group, consider that the prospective member will be armed, and your life and the lives of your loved ones may depend on them.

Induction Interviews

This Handbook is not a definitive source on the subject, but here are a few ideas on induction interviews.

Begin with simple questions such as, Why do you want to join? A good answer is, "To defend peace and justice in our town". A response such as, "To kill Commies" definitely needs follow-up questions, and "I'm sick and tired of being pushed; I want to do the pushing!" is disqualifying.

One reason we need Militia is because too many officials of all kinds either begin with dominance or cruelty issues, or become arrogant with power. We must avoid becoming like those whom we should be arresting.

"What skills or resources can you contribute?" is a good question because the answers suggest where to put the new recruit if admitted. Of course, claims of skills may be falsified; but they can be checked.

Hypothetical questions can be useful. "What would you do if you overheard a city councilman arranging for a bribe from a contractor, or witnessed the mayor ordering a business to close, or customers to leave the premises?". "Shoot the bastard!" is a wrong answer.

How we respect the rights of those we believe to be in the wrong or even committing a crime, indicates how strongly we believe in the rule of law. It also indicates our own level of humility; awareness that we too can make mistakes.

Answers that include individual violent action may be acceptable if the action is intended to halt immediate harm, but the right procedure is:

1) Recognize the problem

2) Halt any violence

3) Secure the situation and evidence for appropriate legal action

Obviously, if another party has initiated violence, and violence is the only available way to halt it and minimize loss of life, violence can be the necessary answer.

Militia Unit Discipline

Maintaining appropriate discipline among members is essential. This does not mean stone faces and spit-shined jackboots, but does mean regular attendance at training events, showing up for work assignments, and refraining from any actions that may bring danger to the public or risk, suspicion, or discredit to the Militia. Such actions may include inappropriate posts on social media, brawling or public intoxication, making unauthorized statements that may be construed as reflecting the attitude or position of the Militia as a whole, or any form of bullying or disrespect ("I'm in the Militia, you had better listen to me!"). Strict safety protocols around handling of firearms, vehicles, and other potentially dangerous materials and equipment must be taught, learned, and practiced.

Members should not take Militia unit equipment on a private hunting trip without proper purpose and authorization, or fail to maintain equipment after a training event.

The leadership of your Militia must establish and follow a consistent procedure for dealing with such problems. Members and mutual goodwill are Militia's most vital possessions, so the procedures must be absolutely fair, calm, sober, and directed whenever possible toward understanding the error and learning from it so as to prevent recurrence.

If your vetting procedure is good, occasions where a member simply reveals incorrigible bad character or judgement should be rare. However persons who may be a hazard to other members or to the community for any reason, or who may bring discredit on the organization, must be ejected.

After all the negative stuff, it should be emphasized that a vital function of the membership officer or committee is to support members, to encourage them, to help them see Militia as a second family, that appreciates and assists them and their families, as well as demanding service and sacrifice. Cookouts, classes, sing-alongs, dances, barn-raisings, hog-butchering, wedding receptions, and birthday parties have been largely lost from our community life today, and should be revived as important parts of the Militia-as-community culture that we must build.

Opportunities for young people to tag along, participate within their abilities, and to learn good citizenship (and good 'adulthood') from adults practicing it, are all vital to preserving our culture. It must be a top priority to provide this social glue and heritage wherever possible.

CHAPTER 2
Intelligence & Communication

If not the most important function, intelligence is surely the one without which the Militia cannot operate to any good purpose: its eyes, ears, nose, and sensitive fingertips. Nothing can be done unless you know what *needs* to be done and the conditions, surroundings, opportunities and difficulties to be encountered in doing it. Beginning a response too late guarantees failure..*Intelligence* is the process of acquiring facts, and turning them into understanding.

Communication is the nervous system integrating the body of Militia, and connecting it to the world around it. These functions need distinct assignments on the leadership team, to assure that they get their deserved attention.

Intelligence

Intelligence-gathering functions of Militia can't be left to chance; they must be a well-thought-out, methodically-applied activity. Information that must be gathered and kept current includes:

- Belief systems and probable intentions of any significant actors in the Area of Operation (AO)

- Movements (ongoing & planned) of any groups or forces relevant to the community

- Intentions of outside groups (government entities, criminal entities, refugees, illegal alien camps, gangs, etc) that may threaten the safety, resources, or rights of the community

- Current & future disposition and availability of resources necessary to the health of the community and operations of the Militia.

- Intelligence sharing with other groups is a core function.

Techniques and resources necessary to this process include first and foremost, good relationships with people in a position to know what the Militia needs to know. This includes good relationships with other similar groups in surrounding areas. Your Militia should regularly monitor Internet sources, relevant publications, public-service and commercial radio and television, and private radio traffic.

Public records of property ownership and of legal proceedings, and public meetings of governing bodies, are very useful intelligence-gathering patrols. In certain situations, surveillance of transportation corridors may be necessary.

Intelligence is an ancient, intricate trade. Raw information is not the same as intelligence, and this small book will not attempt to teach it. Militia groups should seek out members already trained in this craft – and be sure that they're on the side of The People and Constitution!

Communicate, or Not?

Without comms, Militia is a blind dog, able to bark but not knowing what or where to bite, or how to keep the front leg from tripping the back one.

Today, we communicate incessantly and effortlessly face-to-face, by land and cell-phones, snail- and e-mail, and many other Internet-based apps, and via local and national newspapers and magazines. Most of these can be used as convenient, necessary communications within and between Militia units. Subjects for such comms include recruitment, training, muster and event notifications, and planning *alternative* comms.

A significant number of militias and individual preppers and patriots take great pains to operate in secrecy; attempting to be invisible to perceived threats. However, remember the structure of American government, on page 9. The safety of our communities and of Militia and its members *cannot* be guaranteed by hiding; it *must* be secured by numbers and cooperation. Any significant fraction of We the People, organized and trained, is more than a match for any force that can be brought against us. And again: in our form of government where the law-abiding People are the highest level of government, the very *essence* of lawfulness and duty is to be armed and organized. Secrecy is the enemy of trust, and of recruitment.

Loose Lips Sink Ships

However, in law enforcement and other potentially adversarial situations, some information (specific plans and operations, capabilities, or locations) could seriously threaten the effectiveness of a Militia or safety of its members and community if it got into the wrong hands.

We all tend to be proud of what we know, what we are doing, what we have, what we are planning. Among friends, we want to share it all. But in any environment with potential to be hostile (that can be almost everywhere), it is best to develop the habit of asking, "What good purpose will I serve by saying what I want to say?" Even if sharing a piece of information seems good and harmless, is it *necessary?*

Benjamin Franklin is supposed to have said, "One can keep a secret, if he but tell no one. Two can keep a secret, if the one hath not told the other. Three can keep a secret, if two of them are dead."

In hostile or potentially hostile circumstances, you must decide on a policy to control access to information. Again, remember that Militia is not a government or spook agency; it must be coextensive with the community. Secrecy is the enemy of trust, and trust is the lifeblood of every community. The flip side of secrecy is clarity and precision. If you are working with others, is it essential that everyone understand their own part of the operation fully, precisely, and timely.

Austere Comms

The trouble with most normal means of communication mentioned above, is that they need infrastructure that cannot be operated and secured locally. Militia must be able to operate efficiently without 'the grid', and potentially under disapproval or hostility of rogue elements in government or other powerful interests. Therefore, Militia must plan and practice for all needed types of operational comms by means that are sustainable, independent, relatively secure, and under our control.

Radio of various types must be the backbone of this. The technical characteristics of radio communication require different equipment for communication under different conditions and over different distances. Radio comm will be needed over short ranges of feet to furlongs in active operations; over distances of a few to dozens of miles to keep track of needs and events in your county or AO; and over hundreds to thousands of miles to keep abreast of threats or other developments planned in, or approaching from, other States or regions.

This is not a handbook of technical radio operations. Learn from your members who are military veterans or radio users and hobbyists, your local ham radio club, and AMRRON. They will help you to prepare radio capability. You will need it.

There are older communication techniques that should not be ignored. A fire or smoke from a certain hilltop can have a meaning agreed-on in advance. The same with horns, whistles, or sirens. Heliographing (light flashes from the sun reflected by a mirror, used as Morse or other code) can work over many miles, under the right conditions. Drop locations, either 'dead' (unmanned) or live (occupied home, business, etc) can be places where spoken messages or physical recordings of information (flash drives or papers) can be left for retrieval.

Security can be improved, or destroyed by such techniques. Encryption is not infallible, but the fact that encryption is being used, is itself information that you may not wish to reveal.

Another of many subjects not in this book, is codes. We mentioned Morse code; being old and widely known, it is not secure unless of course it is unobserved. Secrecy in communications is vital for some operations. Simpler is almost always better. Extensive planning and diligent practice improves proficiency at any type of comms and reduces the number of things that must be said. A message you do not need to send, cannot be compromised.

Four Contexts for Communication

First: It may seem obvious, but keeping members up to date on Militia business such as training events, community needs and tasks, and to foster camaraderie within the group.

Second: the 'liaison' function, which should be channeled through a specific individual or committee, involves logistical and operational communications and coordination between Militia groups and between the group and other agencies (local, state, and federal governments, paid law enforcement, public service agencies).

For example, official information exchanges and requests for assistance between Militia groups, and between Militia groups and paid police agencies, should be handled by liaison officers. This reduces the chance of information going astray and of conflicting, incorrect, or unreliable information. It also keeps the chain of command intact, so morale and effectiveness are not damaged by conflicting orders. Official reports or requests between the Militia and its county governing body should be handled by its liaison officer. Besides ensuring that information is approved and correct, it minimizes prying and micro-management into the affairs of the Militia by agencies of government.

Third: public information/public relations. Unlike paid forces, again, remember that Militia is We the People. So everyone has a right to know and be a part of what we're doing; but some of our duties, like arresting criminals or successfully repelling an attacker sometimes require that our operations not be fully open to all eyes. While correct knowledge of who we are and what we're doing is usually best for recruitment and gaining public support, information carelessly expressed can be destructively misinterpreted.

Thoughtfully control how you distribute any information related to the Militia.

All members must recognize that while telling the neighbor, "We're training at the park today" is probably harmless, mentioning the skills, maneuvers, or weapons to be covered in the training is possibly *not* harmless. "We're going on an op tonight", even though non-specific, is also not a good idea, and "We're gonna bust the meth lab at the old warehouse!", is likely to cause exactly the wrong kind of surprise.

Information releases should be thoughtfully planned by Militia leadership for clearly articulated good reasons. The task of making information releases should belong exclusively to the Public Relations or Public Information Officer (PIO). Especially under the present, highly lawless, corrupt, vindictive government, specific and approved language should always be used. The PIO must refrain from answering questions for which he has not been prepared and authorized.

Even members of leadership should refer questions from public and media to the PIO, unless a different procedure has been decided upon in advance. Questions of an operational or official nature from other Militia groups or from agencies of government are handled by the Liaison Officer, if the Militia unit is large enough that PIO and Liaison Officer are not the same person.

Fourth: Operational or field comms. This is the moment-by moment exchange of tactical information, orders, condition reports, requests for aid or backup, information on opposing forces, etc, that is exchanged during actual operations. The operations may be hostile and kinetic in character, or may be distributing food, removing storm debris, rescuing persons or animals from hazardous areas or situations, hauling supplies, or surveillance and patrol.

Security of communication is relatively unimportant in disaster relief operations, but paramount in hostile situations. This is where diligent pre-planning and rigorous training can pay off by minimizing the amount of talk and the level of detail required. Coded or digital transmission, low radiated power, directional beaming, and many other techniques can be used to minimize leakage of information and also minimize the chances the transmissions will allow the opposing force to locate you. Making your transmissions as brief as possible, as weak as possible (low power means you are less likely to be heard from far away) and as few as possible, will go a long way to keeping your unit safe in the field.

And *keep it simple;* the fancier and more complicated your codes, equipment, and procedures, the likelier they are to fail at the worst moment.

The Communications and/or Liaison Officers, and other personnel responsible for communications need not be experts in the technical aspects of comms equipment and its operation. But if they are not, they're responsible to find training or develop the required technical experts to work with/under them. This division of responsibility can be a good thing because often, the thoughtful, well-spoken person who is adroit with words is not tech-savvy, and the reverse is true. Many tech-savvy people are not good at communicating with people.

One more thing this book is not, is a course in physics of radio or communication security techniques. But there is a large literature on the subject, and many people who are trained in it. *Seek out the information now, before you need it and can't access it.*

CHAPTER 3

Logistics

Logistics refers to materials and transportation. The military aphorism, *"Get there the firstest with the mostest"* describes a triumph of logistics.

The Logistics function includes planning and overseeing all movement of personnel, materiel, and equipment; planning, acquisition and protection, and inventory maintenance of all supplies and equipment. This includes firearms and ammunition (everyone's first thought), but also more importantly: food, water, vehicles, fuels, medical supplies and equipment, clothing, tools, powered transport, perhaps bicycles, horses or other pack animals, and all other materiel belonging to or used by the Militia.

Effective logistics function is essential to success in the field of any Militia action, and also essential to judging feasibility of any operation during the planning process. Responsibility for logistics functions should be delineated in your leadership structure.

Our accustomed permissive-environment thinking, "Just throw it in the truck and go", or "Stop by Wal-Mart on the way and get some" is likely to be impractical or impossible in hostile conditions and makes us predictable, which under hostile conditions can make us ineffective, or *dead.*

Logistics sub-functions are 1) inventory; 2) corridors, routes and terrain; 3) transportation modes; 4) transportation equipment and operators; and 5) time.

Inventory: Includes all the things the Militia may need for sustenance and operation…water, food, clothes, weapons, ammo, repair parts, fuel for heating and vehicles, demolition devices and materials, batteries and charging systems for vehicles, night-vision, radios, computers, tires, etc.

It is essential that the entire leadership team collaborate to develop a comprehensive inventory/shopping list of everything the Militia may need, so the Logistics officer can develop sources, stocks, and management practices for these items. Of course, the things we may need depends on what we expect to need to do; so the planning process is large and inclusive. It can't be divided into areas like logistics or materiel until the overall Militia unit planning is complete (what operations to expect).

Every item in the inventory has size, weight and transportability, cost, degree of fragility and perishability, storage requirements, load and unload procedures and needed equipment (cranes, forklifts, ramps?), quantities likely needing to be transported, perhaps need to conceal or disguise, and occasionally equipment needed for storage, such as refrigeration. Under ordinary conditions each item has one or more sources, but may need to be sought from alternative sources if conditions change, or may need to be stockpiled against unobtainability (e.g., ammunition). .

Each Militia inventory item has a degree of urgency with which it is likely to be needed. That affects where they should be stored relative to where they are likely to be needed. Spreadsheets can be used to organize this information for inventory items, but the information may need to be accessed under hostile or emergency conditions, so consider hard copy or hardened computer systems. Nothing can substitute for a diligent Logistics officer or team.

Corridors, routes, and terrain: To develop an adequate working knowledge of relevant corridors, routes, and terrain, even a small AO must be divided into distinct **regions** of different characters, within and among which movement may be required.

For instance, your AO may contain these: on a lake, Northern lake shore, Southern lake shore, Northern and Southern edges of Town (for each town in AO), business district(s), industrial areas, government buildings, housing developments, farming areas, mountain areas, etc. Each area has different opportunities and obstacles for movement in, out, and within. They will be interconnected or separated by navigable or unnavigable water; by roads of different sizes; perhaps by rail; by underground utility corridors; by pedestrian or bike paths; by walls and fences; and by more or less difficult overland routes.

Valleys, highways, local roads, unimproved roads, logging roads, hiking trails, railroad tracks, navigable waters, meadows fields or prairies, open forest, even sewer or electrical or mine tunnels can all be thought of as **corridors** along which personnel and materials can move. Each corridor has advantages and disadvantages for moving different things to different places by different types of equipment. Access by air must be considered, both supporting and hostile.

Similar information must be collected, perhaps at a lower level of detail, for the area surrounding the AO. This is because the unit may have to travel to assist other groups, because materiel or assistance may have to be bought in to the AO, and because threats of different kinds may enter. Study *in advance* routes by which these may take place, and how these routes may be obstructed, by a hostile force or by you..

Obviously, maps are essential. Waste no time in obtaining them, since availability may become subject to restriction, if doing so is seen to offer a tactical advantage to a hostile party able to do so.

Typical large-scale highway maps may be sufficient to orient you to places hundreds of miles away from your AO. But you must know much better the areas where you may have to travel and operate. U.S. Geological Survey 7½ minute quadrangle topographic maps each covering an area roughly 7x8 miles. If you have access to a large color printer you can make your own from online data. For the rest of your State outside your AO, DeLorme publishes state atlases of topo maps that are much less detailed but still indicate topography, watercourses, and even minimally-improved roads.

If possible, all the maps of a given area used by your unit should be identical, same edition, so that in communications you can refer to features and locations by their coordinate position on the map, and you do not have to name them or give latitude and longitude. This adds some security to your comms, as an eavesdropper would need to have an identical map to discover the locations you refer to.

Transportation modes:

Water needs to be broken down further into shallow or deep, quiet or rough water for long or short distances;

Land needs to be broken down further into good road, poor road, cross-country, firm and level, swamp or mountain, man-powered, animal-powered, engine-powered; or perhaps even rail, pipeline, or even funicular (rope/cord/cable).

Air transport must be broken down, depending on size, quantity and weight of items to be moved, facilities for takeoff and landing, availability of aircraft, pilots, special fuels or maintenance;

Equipment and Operators: Equipment that can, and may need to be, used for transport includes pockets, backpacks, bicycles, cars, buses, trucks, and drones; farm, construction, mining, and logging equipment; kayaks, canoes, inflatables, boats, yachts and barges; and aircraft of all types. Specialized, attack-resistant military-type equipment is unlikely to be available to Militia, but civilian equipment can be creatively adapted and is cheaper and inconspicuous. Depending on the characteristics of the AO and types of equipment likely to be needed and available, you should make a priority of training members in applicable operating and maintenance skills, and/or recruit members with these skills.

Equipment belonging to the Militia or its members and designated for Militia use must be maintained to a high level to assure availability. Consider modification to improve capabilities and reliability if your Militia has access to the necessary skills. Stock spare tires and other parts likely to need replacement, and any special tools needed. Fuel supply and conservation must be planned. Also consider choosing or modifying vehicles for EMP resistance.

Time: is of the essence in any emergent or hostile environment. The logistics officer must study available equipment, likely loads, and the AO, so as to be able to accurately plan time needed to move whatever to wherever, under all sorts of conditions. Google Travel Planner will not cut it.

CHAPTER 4

Training

Training is everything that must be done to ensure that members will have the skills, knowledge, mindset and habits or experience needed to accomplish their share of any mission. Since the overall mission of Militia includes a wide variety of essential sub-tasks, the list of potentially desirable subjects for training is almost limitless.

Training cannot be left to whim and opportunity. Responsibility for training must be assigned, and must coordinate with overall planning functions to assure that skills will be present to execute operations.

We must observe in passing that our Constitution requires, in Article I Section 8 Clause 16, that the States provide for, 'training the Militia according to the discipline prescribed by Congress'. If that were happening, this book might not need to exist.

Militia operates within its community, so the line between in-house and outsourced skills or services can be fuzzy. In general, any skill or service Militia needs that is not urgent, that is not needed in the kinetic tactical environment, can be brought in from the community.

The skills that cannot wait, that cannot be outsourced for reasons of operational security (OPSEC), that are integral to the Militia's constitutional duties, or that are not easily found in the community, must be taught and maintained in-house.

The skills needed by Militia fill many books. They can be found from many sources and are offered by many professional trainers. In Appendix G we provide an incomplete list compiled by a military veteran, mostly focused on confrontational skills. But here we will engage in a broader necessarily incomplete discussion of subjects, in which your group should seek or provide training.

First bear in mind that training is an activity. In peaceful times it will be Militia's *main* activity. As with firefighting, you do not need it...until you *need* it. Being together and working together creates group cohesion; *esprit de corps*. Training meetings should be regular, predictable, and you should plan and announce them far enough in advance that members can work them into their schedules.

Just as well-run churches do, your Militia should seek to involve entire families in training activities. Of course, not all of the Militia's duties are suitable for all family members; but inclusion will minimize the ambivalence and family stress that arises if Militia duty is seen as in conflict with family time. We know that we participate in Militia to protect our families, but if wives and children feel we are abandoning them to train with the guys, at best we'll show up for training less often. Also, the better our families understand what we're doing and absorb skills too, the better they will support this duty in both quiet and trying times.

They will also be better able to take care of themselves, and even provide help when conditions require. Remember 'tooth-to-tail' ratio: to keep operating, every operator needs many people behind him in service and support functions.

Skills for Conflict: Military and Tactical

An important general principle for all training: specialization is necessary for some functions because of unique abilities needed, depth of training required to develop them, and/or heavy workload; but all personnel should know as much as possible and each member must be able to do as many jobs as possible. This brings diverse perspectives and experience to tasks.

Knowing more of the big picture increases the member's sense of involvement in the organization and helps him do his job better by understanding how it fits. Most importantly, it makes the Militia more effective and resilient because injury or absence of one or a few members will not eliminate their capabilities. *Cross-train!*

Again, the literature of military science is vast and old, and we will not attempt to duplicate it here. This section will list and briefly describe subject areas in which you should seek information, but we will not provide much of it here.

Health

The foundation of operational effectiveness is the human participant, and his or her health is the basis for existence.

The spiritual is the source of the physical. So although it may sound odd in a materialist and secular culture, training for spiritual health should be a conscious process. I do not suggest that explicitly religious instruction should have any official place in Militia training; but we ourselves and everything we see are manifestations of God's existence, purpose, and love. Each of us has a definite role or duty within that purpose. If it were not so, we would not be here. The moral law (of God) is as real and binding as the natural law (of God; like gravity). These facts undergirding our Constitution and civilization are powerful aids to morale in difficult times, and indispensable guides for good choices in stressful and confusing circumstances.

As shy as most people are about being instructed about matters of spiritual health, many are shyer still about the physical. Most people today have a vague awareness that the way they live and eat affects their health, but changing even obviously unhealthy habits is difficult because we fall into them for powerful psychological reasons. The last excuse is "It's *my* life"; but in the Militia context that's untrue. We are in Militia because we recognize a duty to God, our families, and our community.

Neglecting our health by failing to exercise and by eating garbage ultimately goes beyond merely reducing our effectiveness. It makes us a burden on those around us. In a dangerous world, this is no less than dereliction of our duty to care for those around us. Everybody expects PT (physical training) in the form of running, push-ups, sit-ups, etc, to be a part of Militia exercise. If we are serious about being true servants to God and our community, we must attend to the foundation as well as the more visible upper stories of the building. In an increasingly unhealthy world, never mind making life longer and more pleasant; superior fitness can be a decisive *tactical* advantage.

Adaptability

We've discussed logistics and intelligence; both are essential in hostile and friendly environments. A hostile environment or active opposition changes and adds burden to both functions. Restrictions on information sources and movement, disinformation, the need to avoid observation, and time-sensitivity are the most significant differences.

Tools

Weapons applications, use, and maintenance are a core area in which Militia must develop competence. Rifles and pistols are fundamental and must be the personal property of each member. They should meet an appropriate group standard and be maintained to that standard. The group can either supply standard weapons to members unable to afford their own, or raise funds from the community to do so.

With or without diversity of personal weapons, members should train in operation and maintenance of as wide a variety of weapons as possible. Familiarity with a variety of weapons that may be encountered in the hands of allies or opponents, is highly desirable. Knowing capabilities and weaknesses of weapons can make the difference between success and failure of an operation, or between life and death, helping you avoid injury by an opponent's weapon and by being able to assist in the use of an ally's; or by allowing you to pick up and use one left by an opponent. Consider the value of recruiting one or more gunsmiths or armorers into your group. Seek out NRA or Appleseed Project classes.

Traditional martial arts training if available should be a part of the physical training program. Regardless of the particular school, any of them is beneficial as a mind-discipline, as well as enhancing the ability to prevail in silence without weapons when that is necessary or desirable.

Tactical field operations, emphasizing small-unit and guerilla techniques, should be studied and practiced. Your AO will suggest some specialization in certain types of operation (mountain, swamp, desert, winter, waterborne, urban, suburban).

Guerilla and militia operations differ from operations conducted by nation-states in many ways, especially frugality. Neither unlimited human cannon-fodder nor unlimited ammunition is available to small groups fighting a larger opponent, nor will you see any of your members as expendable. This must be reflected in the tactics you train to use.

If instruction in operations and use of heavy weapons systems, military engineering, and demolition is available, it should be a part of your training curriculum. The threat environment you may encounter cannot be predicted. We cannot assume the effectiveness, availability, and loyalty of paid armed forces: our constitutional charge, *"execute the Laws of the Union, suppress Insurrections, and repel Invasions"* is very broad.

Military veterans in your group will be the best sources for most of these types of training. What they do not know, they will be familiar with sources for, in the literature of military science.

Skills for Disaster

Disaster response and relief is not a Constitutional function of Militia. Of course, in the self-reliant, Christian culture of early America, the same men with the same attitude who fought hostile Indians and later the British tyranny, were those who also pulled people from floodwater and rebuilt lightning-burned barns.

Disaster response should be part of your duty as modern Militia, for several reasons. The first is because the primary reason we work together as Militia is our God-ordained duty to serve, to defend our families and protect the weak, to execute God's Law. That Divine mandate covers far more than the formal constitutional charge.

The second reason is that training to serve in disaster response puts us in constructive partnership with the panoply of paid agencies from town police to FEMA, with whom we must come into contact as Militia: sometimes to cooperate, sometimes to discipline. *The better we know them and they know us, the more constructive and successful those encounters will be.*

The third reason is that our effectiveness depends on the relationship we cultivate in our own communities with our neighbors. The more they come to correctly see us as trusted helpers, the more they will support us politically when we deal with government, and the more they will support us practically with food, encouragement, refuge, information, concealment, and membership.

Predictable Disaster

Contrary to its image, disaster is very predictable. Everyone knows that low-lying areas flood; that forests burn; that volcanoes erupt; that electricity fails; that deep snow falls and strong winds blow; that sicknesses can spread. There are well-known ways to deal with every type of disaster; the only thing that is not known is exactly when these things will happen, and to what degree. We also know that the severity of the human outcome depends as much on the degree of human preparedness, as on the intensity of the disaster.

This handbook section is about training, not about operations, so once again we will not attempt to duplicate or condense the enormous literature of disaster response and preparedness. We will only suggest things you should consider, trusting that your unit will find and use existing educational resources.

A responsible attitude toward a dangerous world is, look in all directions. Among your members who are alert to political, legal, and societal risks, you will surely have a few who are planning for the physical ones: the 'preppers'. Your leadership team will decide how much the prepper mindset will guide curriculum, but they definitely should be among your instructors, and they will recommend other resources on the subject.

There are government agencies such as FEMA offering training in many types of emergency management and disaster response. Have one of your members find out what is being offered near you through your local government's emergency response office, through your sheriff, or direct from FEMA. You may dislike the agencies involved or disagree with the material taught. You may doubt the long-term value of much of the material since it relies on disaster being localized, and assistance and materials being abundantly available from outside a circumscribed disaster area.

But you will learn something, and the certifications your group members receive will provide credibility and new ways to cooperate with the official apparatus, connect them with new sources of intelligence, give them uncontested access to places you would otherwise be barred from, and further enhance your group's reputation and credibility in your community.

The behavior and availability of structures plays a crucial role in disaster and disaster recovery; so recruit builders, carpenters, masons, welders, heavy equipment operators, and engineers as Militia members, to employ their skills and spread them as much as possible.

Skills for Law Enforcement & Conflict Resolution

To 'execute the Laws' in the words of the Constitution, implies knowing the Law. In the modern sense of enforcing criminal law, the Grand Jury with its open-ended investigative power must be Militia's guide; and Militia with its physical power is Grand Jury's sword.

However, Militia's duty to execute Law goes beyond the methodical processes of bringing criminals into the justice system. Law, we must remember, derives first from God's Law which orders the universe and prescribes our relations with Him, with each other, and with the rest of His Creation. Upon that foundation, human Law exists, paraphrasing our Declaration of Independence, to secure the rights He gave us, against invasion by other fallen men.

Securing individual rights in the moment may involve putting a head-lock on a convenience-store robber; sitting in the bushes outside the house of the ex-wife of a serial abuser; having a very long conversation with a vaccination-enforcement team from the state palace, at a roadblock outside your town; or putting a bullet in the head of a kidnapper as he runs away with a screaming child. But are you sure that the child was not bitten by a snake, and the man is not Daddy, rushing him to the hospital?

So we see that properly executing the Law requires much knowledge, discernment, cool thinking, forbearance...and training, so that we will react correctly in the moment.

Legal training for Militia should begin with Law's beginning, God's Law, and the Constitution. The Internet is full of sites and people teaching the Bible, the Constitution, and their application.

Don't trust just one or two to give you the whole story or correct perspective. Remember, We the People have primary authority over all branches of government[3], to interpret and apply the Constitution[3]. This means that we must study, think deeply, be humble, and careful; *not* act haughty and autocratic.

Constant consultations among group leaders and with leaders of other groups, as well as with your county's TACTICAL CIVICS™ chapter or other Constitutionalist support organization, even with spiritual leaders, are vital to understanding the implications of new developments.   Do not scorn the knowledge of professional attorneys, police officers, and judges; just remember that these people work together daily, making their living from the application of the law. In the case of attorneys and judges, their living is enhanced when they can make the law seem more frightening and obscure. So their perspective on it may not be in accord with Law's primary legitimate purpose in our Republic: to secure the rights of individuals.

Four types of Law-Enforcement Activity

Militia's Constitutional law-enforcement activity will mostly fall into four categories.

First: It is merely every person's obligation to oppose evil where they see it. Intervene in robberies, stop car-jackings or muggings, stop purse-snatchers, halt beatings, and church shootings. We see news clips about such happenings. The NRA gathers and re-tells stories about 'The Armed Citizen'. "None of my business…don't want to get involved" is not an acceptable attitude for one who stands up in his godly and constitutional role as defender of his community.

Such crime-stopping actions will usually be individual, not organized actions of multiple Militia members. But your Militia should provide training to render its members more effective in such situations. Situational awareness and safe, swift, accurate firearms

____

3

The People Themselves, Kramer, pg. 248

handling are important, as are unarmed techniques. The principle of "appropriate use of force" is vital: never unnecessarily escalate a situation. If you are near enough, and strong and skilled enough, to halt a crime in progress with a grab, lock, or throw, do not bring out a weapon.

It is better still when you can de-escalate a situation with words. These techniques should be part of Militia's training curriculum.

Second: assistance to paid law enforcement agencies. Depending on the relationship your group has developed with them, and your level of skills and training, you may mostly be called on to assist with traffic control, neighborhood watch, or possibly prisoner transport. Or you may be asked to provide firepower and tactical or strategic support in kinetic operations against drug or other powerful gangs. *Because your constitutional charge includes suppressing insurrections and repelling invasions, no level of military operation is beyond the potential purview of Militia.*

If your membership is suited to it and you have, or can develop, sources of advanced military training, seriously consider it. Sources can include military veterans in your membership and their contacts, published literature, and professional tactical trainers.

Your relationships with paid law enforcement units and their appreciation of your ability to help, will give your group access to training and facilities through them in the specific skills they need from you; another reason to diligently cultivate these relationships.

Third: enforcement of the rights of your community members against potential usurpations by rogue servants in government. This may involve standing at the door of a restaurant to prevent disruption of its business by lawless mandates, blocking road access to your county by agencies intending to violate the rights of residents, or halting execution of a 'red flag' confiscation order.

This type of operation will be the most delicate the Militia will ever have to conduct; because it involves likely confrontation between opposing armed elements who both believe that the law is on their side. It has the greatest potential to escalate catastrophically out of control. And because government agencies can be downright treacherous when their PR is on the line, it carries the greatest risk of injuring the public's view of Militia upholding the Constitution.

This is when advance intelligence, negotiating and de-escalating skills, knowledge of the law, robust, geographically wide networks of mutual support, AND your community's confidence in your unit are most important.

To plan the successful defense of your rights against rogue official agencies, you need time, which requires advance warning, which requires a robust intelligence gathering and analysis capability. The best confrontation is the one that never happens, therefore early contact should be made with the agency of concern, to convince them to stay within the Law and not attempt to violate it. Negotiating techniques to keep communication clear and open are vital to avoid mucking it up with ego conflict or unnecessary offensiveness.

Also vital is accurate knowledge of the Law, to explain to the agency what is actually required of it. Wide networks of support facilitate intel gathering, and also make it clear that your opposition to a usurpation is not a minor local phenomenon but has broad popular, geographic, and if necessary, tactical support.

Your first response to intel that a serious invasion on individual rights by an official actor is planned must be widely-publicized statements, in every possible public medium as well as directed to the command structure from which the threat emanates, explaining clearly its illegality and appealing for reversal of the plan; appealing also for conscientious, oath-keeping disobedience to it on the part of all personnel likely to be involved under the lawless orders.

This "first' response must be tirelessly and deafeningly repeated, continuously, until the threat is gone, even if other actions must be initiated.

The second level of response must be preparation to physically interdict the invasion. That may take various forms, and should be planned to take place as early in the process as possible, including   disabling   the   invasion   force   at   its   base.

Every physical action must be accompanied by repetition of the "first response".

Physical obstruction of the invasion at the State, County, or other legally and tactically appropriate boundary, does not just mean roadblocks or other physical interdiction. Once again, face-to-face exhortation to the personnel of the invading force (if they are fellow Americans) must be made, giving them *every* opportunity to obey the law, defy their unlawful orders, stand down, turn around, before their progress is resisted with potentially lethal force. Promise, and be prepared to provide, protection for those who do the right thing

If resources do not exist for a credible physical resistance to the invasion *per se*, or if such resistance fails, then it becomes the obligation of the Militia to lead a continuing underground resistance, assuring to the extent possible the necessities of life and safety to the occupied population, and all possible continuing obstruction of and interference with the unlawful activities of the invader.

At the same time, appeals to law and public opinion must continue, until Constitutional freedom and security are re-established and the criminal invaders are submitted to the due process of law.

War-gaming such situations and consultation with a wide range of like-minded groups is vital, and will inform training requirements for such operations. You should develop redundant specialists in negotiating, law, public information, and in agency hierarchies, resources, and geographic distribution.

Fourth: in the long term, Militia's most important law enforcement function is arresting and deterring official crime. It is the greatest threat our civilization faces today. Remember that four times as many people were murdered by their own governments, as were killed in wars between 1914 and 1991[4]

4

Death by Government, R.J. Rummel (Transaction, 1994)

Such activity will almost exclusively be in close coordination with, and in the service of, your Grand Jury. They will investigate individuals and agencies for criminal invasions of rights, financial fraud and misappropriation of resources, bribery, and other crimes. But the Grand Jury will need Militia to execute its search and arrest warrants and subpoenas. This should be a peaceful white-collar activity, however it may encounter evasion or physical opposition.

Expertise in handling evidence to preserve its validity in court is crucial, or major criminals can walk because your unit mishandled the evidence. Observing the rights of the subjects of the processes that you execute is also vital (Grand Jury witnesses and targets do not have the right to an attorney; that is for the trial stage only). Militia must always be about rule of law; we must set the highest example, even with individuals we believe to be the worst actors.

Having the County Ordinances enacted establishes your Militia's constitutional legitimacy and is absolutely prerequisite for both the third and fourth types of activity. The type of lawless activities by rogue agencies that we discussed obstructing above, can be arrested peacefully before they begin, if the criminal intent of rogue officials is discovered and prosecuted early. Militia, via its intel network, will often be able to provide *presentments* to the Grand Jury, which will in turn have Militia execute its warrants. For a glimpse into what may be possible in the not too distant future, read about the proposed Indictment Engine™ mobile app project of the TACTICAL CIVICS™plan

Retired police officers, prosecutors, or judges can be the best teachers of the necessary procedures, and pitfalls to avoid. Of course, relatively few can overcome the institutional prejudices of their careers and the bad attitudes that were part of their training, in order to appreciate your constitutional role, and be willing to support it.

Fools Rush In...

If yours is the first Militia unit in your area to become

Constitutional through our model *Constitution Enforcement and Militia Ordinance,* complemented by the *Grand Jury Ordinance,* you should **not** immediately pursue high-profile official crooks. Continue building your unit's rock-solid reputation by furnishing community service, preparedness education, and helping the paid law enforcement while you *wait* for a few surrounding counties to also pass our model Ordinance.

The first time you try to take down a powerful crook, you *will* encounter resistance (perhaps physical, certainly procedural) as the other rogues in the system back up their comrade with every sort of obstruction tactic and legal-sounding propaganda.

So, you must have backup, too: public awareness and support beyond your own county, other similar simultaneous actions, other Militias and Grand Juries who will follow up on trails that lead out of your jurisdiction. The criminal enterprises you are about to tackle have built themselves up over generations, and are allied from sea to shining sea!

Do not pick the fight until you are prepared to win it. Some ideas on how to counter official obstruction will be found in Appendix E.

Skills for Transportation and Movement

Few people today think seriously about movement without wheels and an engine. Being able to think outside the 'box on wheels' can give you a tactical advantage. You can move silently across terrain that looks impossible, and appear where you're not expected. To do that requires physical training. PT must be a part of Militia for all of its members who are not medically incapable. If you are not fit, you cannot care for your community, and in difficult conditions you will be a burden to it.

On the foundation of physical fitness, build skills like cross-country wayfinding with and without map and compass (GPS should not be relied on); covert camping; planning, packing, and carrying a ruck; cross-country skiing or snowshoeing; urban movement including following targets and losing followers in the maze of streets; cutting across blocks by way of buildings; scaling walls and fences; using subway, utility, or other tunnels; swimming with and without snorkel or SCUBA gear; and use of boats. Concentrate on the types of routes and conditions important to your AO.

Physical fitness is important even to use of vehicles, for swift entry and exit possibly under fire, for loading and unloading cargo, for driving under extreme conditions, and maintaining control when the power-steering belt breaks.

Your group should train in skills to operate as many different types of vehicles as possible. Truck drivers, farmers, heavy equipment operators and four-wheeling enthusiasts will be valuable resources, but do not just let them do it; use them as trainers to spread their skills. Don't let your operation fail because your man on the spot can't drive a 'stick', back up a trailer, use jumper cables, or change a tire.

Route planning for various vehicles, loads, weather and road conditions will usually be a command-level function. But the more of these skills your drivers have, the more adaptable and autonomous they will be, and the more able to complete a mission despite unforeseen circumstances.

Your drivers should know how to load a vehicle, and how to recognize a load that is too heavy, too light, poorly placed, likely to be damaged, or likely to fall off....and how to remedy these problems.

Skills for Community Resilience & Survival

Here is where the preppers in your group can shine; but most preppers are focused on their own family's survival while your Militia's duty is to your whole community. This means that your activities in this direction will be as much education and outreach, as 'planning and piling'.

Preparing to survive disasters: to rebuild, preserve and grow food, learn to live without the electrical grid, and similar things may not at first seem like legitimate Militia activity, but of course, they are. Any invasion, large-scale insurrection, or concerted attempt to subdue patriotic America will involve collapse of conventional supply chains and power and comm grids. To support your ability to fight back, as well as to protect your community, you must plan and prepare to operate independently.

Of course, some areas may not be able to independently supply some needs, and some may only be able to supply very few, depending on population, climate, soils, urbanization, and other factors. What you cannot provide locally, you must trade for; just as happens now. However, rather than simply relying on established supply chains that are not under your control or involve parties whose loyalties you do not know, you must plan robust new ones, with other similar groups and like-minded individuals.

Trade today is usually facilitated by the great convenience of currency, and that may continue to be practicable for your contingency-trading plans. However, currency and its use are potentially subject to various types of control and interruption by illegitimate government, so you should consider what types of direct trades or barter arrangements could be substituted.

Cultivating relationships with local producers is critical. Farmers are obvious; manufacturers may be less obvious, but still vital. Timber and sawmill operators, blacksmiths, gunsmiths, machine shops, fabricators, orchards, bakeries, scrapyards should all be noted, and contacted, about their potential role in supporting your community, and Militia activity, if ordinary supply chains break down.

Area studies are of critical importance. Find out where your town's water for drinking and firefighting comes from; how your sewer plant works, and what are the immediate, and longer-term consequences, if they stop.

Yes, Militia should know these things. Remember that Militia is not an army, directed and supplied from outside, whose sole job is kill and break things. Your are the self-defense, the self-preservation of your community. Neutralizing kinetic threats when they appear naturally takes priority, but Militia's responsibility neither begins nor ends there.

How is fuel brought into your area, and from where? Which

utilities have their own standby power, and how much fuel do they stock? This information will let you map the potential development (spread in space and time) of critical problems for your community if supplies are interrupted.

Again, relief of the population does not seem like your job as Militia, but pain in your community will impact your ability to operate, and may be used as leverage against you by an opposing force.

But you are unlikely to have the resources to do it all. Part of your vital network-building must be to partner with other community groups more specifically organized to address such needs. Most areas have an official emergency-management office, with which your group should develop a relationship, understanding that most such departments depend on aid from other government agencies, which could be interrupted by natural, hostile, or political events.

This sort of planning overlaps with training, because it involves finding and learning from people with all sorts of experience, including logistics, power generation and distribution, food production and distribution, alternative energy and technologies, psychology, economics. Looking at local conditions, resources, obstacles and opportunities through all these lenses is necessary to prepare your Militia for its broad duty.

CHAPTER 5

Leadership & Command

Today's American Militia is an organization with a dual character, and this must be reflected in its organization and governance. We hope that most of the time it meets, trains, and functions as a convivial community organization. Besides assisting with many community functions, being the law-enforcement arm of We the People means that it must stay aware of contemporary legal issues and developments, and develop a well-grounded, robust consensus on them that is firmly grounded in the Constitution and in the Divine Law that inspires and illuminates it.

Deliberative Governance

These are thoughtful, deliberative functions. They require a structure that is open to all ideas and allows time for consideration. This careful philosophical process, the working of the righteous will of We the People, needs to undergird all physical Militia action.

Democratic organization is also the clear tradition of American Militia. Members have always elected and removed their own officers when needed. Militia is, in George Mason's phrase, "the whole People...". This is the same People who enacted our Constitution, the same that assembled In Congress to make our Declaration of Independence.

Thus, all important decisions of and for the Militia must be made by its members in open, deliberative process. Of course members with less appetite for discussion can delegate; but the culture and the organization of the Militia must reflect shared, public exercise of consensus and individual *responsibility*.

Obviously, meetings (real or virtual) are the setting for deliberation, and details of how they are run can vary, as long as everyone has opportunity to speak and be heard, and conclusions are respected by all. Minutes should be taken and preserved to facilitate learning (constructive change) and consistency (holding to the truth). Many bodies use *Robert's Rules of Order,* but fancy parliamentary procedure must neither become an end in itself, nor a tool to impede, derail, obfuscate, or silence.

While decisions and policies must be the will of The People under the Law, it is neither practical to try to force all members to participate in all deliberations, nor does the limited knowledge and appetite for detail of most people support the best decision-making. You will need some form of leaders' council or guidance committee, with elected members representing the distinct areas of expertise and responsibility described above. The sample By-Laws in Appendix C describe such a body and the responsibilities that should be represented on it.

Whether multiple nearby Militia units should have completely separate governance or whether they should pool and concentrate responsibility is a local decision. But if a unit has sufficient membership to fill all of the important areas of expertise listed above, it's large enough to have its own independent governance structure. If the unit is small enough that one person has to wear several hats, it would probably benefit from sharing its governance process with one or more other units. Of course, in sparsely populated areas, distance or diverse conditions may make shared governance undesirable or impractical. Conversely, areas with large, homogeneous populations and common interests can gain efficiency and better-qualified leadership by drawing a single leadership team from multiple units.

Field Command

Field command is the other distinct, necessary form of governance. Once your group decides on operations (directly or through its leadership team), successful execution requires a *non-*deliberative, authoritarian, hierarchical, military-style command structure. Even training events and community services, once planned, should be run in this fashion to maximize efficiency, safety, and precision.

As stated above, it is traditional and essential to justice and unit cohesion and effectiveness, that all officers be chosen, and if necessary, removed, according to clear, definite democratic process. However, their *operational* authority must not be subject to casual discussion or frivolous refusal if you want to execute good plans successfully with minimal loss or collateral damage.

The precise ranks or other details of command structure may be devised by the unit commander with the approval of the unit membership (usually through its leadership team), but should be uniform among units in the same area, or that are likely to work together. Most groups use a sub-set of the traditional military ranks, usually leaving room at the top for large-scale command if Militias are called together to State service. Some use the well-known Incident Command System.

Some people just love complication, hierarchy, fancy uniforms, titles, mandatory forms of address, and elaborate distinctions of rank. These individuals should be sat on, or encouraged to apply for a job with the IRS. Militia is We the People, and our calling is to bring humility before God and our neighbors to the apex human sovereignty in our Republic, and to model devotion to duty; the polar opposite of the tendencies of human power structures.

Similarity of Militia's operational command structures to conventional military command must not be allowed to obscure the profound fact that Militia is not an army. It is not a simple tool of violent destruction, or even of violent defense. No Militiaman is simply a cog, an externally directed part of a chain of command. Remember that Militia is We the People, sovereign not serf. It needs efficient hierarchical operational command, but that must always recognize and must interface with the moral and legal reality of the individual before God, and with the consensus of the community. Even the *Uniform Code of Military Justice* recognizes the fraught obligation to refuse illegal orders, but Militia's responsibility to exercise legal judgement goes far beyond that of a merely military organization.

The field or operational commander or his designee commands all external operations of the Militia of all kinds, and must be ultimately responsible for the highest possible level of personnel and public safety, and for the successful completion of the operation. All military, quasi-military, law-enforcement, and training operations should be under the exclusive command of the operational commander and his subordinates.

CHAPTER 6

Partnerships

As Militia is a function of The People as a whole, the more inclusive and open it is – the better it communicates about its history, mandates, structure, function, activities and operations – the better. Many of us give a great deal of thought to grave events we see looming which may plunge us into civil war; thus, our attention is on secrecy, mistrust, misdirection, camouflage, and tactical surprise. These are tools for conflict, so they must be kept sharp.

But necessary attention to them must not taint the essential spiritual nature of Militia, which is the good men of the community, shoulder to shoulder, grateful and humble in the high duty with which God has blessed them, in joyful camaraderie and mutual trust, taking care of business.

The spirit of partnership should extend in all possible directions. Any business in the community should be brought to appreciate the value to itself, in its employees' participation. In turn, it should seize the opportunity to support its community's Militia.

Militia should approach schools and colleges in the area with offers of help in marksmanship, martial arts, physical conditioning, orienteering, wilderness travel, extreme driving, and any other classes or programs in which your Militia unit can furnish or point to useful expertise.....not to mention security.

Churches and other community groups should be shown how Militia can assist them with security, security planning, victimization prevention, and mere manpower for community-wide disasters or events affecting only one or a few families, such as fires, downed trees, or landslides.

The fire companies, rescue squads, FEMA offices, and any other first response organizations probably will have shared membership with your Militia. But cooperation and coordination should also be official, and close. Militia members without specific first-response skills can still make valuable contributions in the form of traffic control, clerical, maintenance, commissary, or other services.

The Boys in Blue, Black, Tan, or Gray

Even before your governing body enacts our model *Constitution Enforcement and Militia Ordinance,* (Appendix A) making it official, your Militia should pursue a good working relationship with all the paid law-enforcement agencies in your AO. These are usually understaffed for the tasks expected of them. If you take care to cultivate the relationship, soon they won't believe how they ever functioned without Militia backup.

Your community will realize significant benefit in terms of better crime prevention and response, from this partnership. But potentially more important, is the opportunity that mutual trust and familiarity will provide, to peacefully resolve any situations in which corrupt leadership attempts to use paid law enforcement to infringe the People's rights.

Nothing is gained by rubbing the noses of the paid agencies (who have much more experience at the job than Militia does) in

Militia's superior Constitutional legitimacy. Yet, the only law-enforcement specified in the Constitution is the Militia, and it is vital that close association with the sometimes-arrogant paid agencies *not* taint Militia's devotion to the Law that is the creation, servant, and defense of We the People.

Ancient and Essential

Militia's most important partner in law-enforcement is the other ancient, pre-constitutional, Common Law institution carried into our system: the Grand Jury, the subject of Volume 2 in the Tactical Civics (TM) series of which the first edition of this book was originally part..

What is essential for Militia to know about this partnership is that, except for instances where crime-in-progress is actually witnessed by Militia members and must be immediately stopped, Militia's power of the sword *must* be guided by the investigatory, fact-finding power of the Grand Jury. Militia, in turn, provides hands, feet, and force if necessary to execute Grand Jury's warrants, and to maintain the security and anonymity of Grand Jury members and the secrecy of their process, lest powerful criminals intimidate or eliminate them.

CHAPTER 7

If Not Now, When? If Not You, Who?

This book has been a long time coming, but a rather short

time ripening. Events in our world now urgently demand of every decent, responsible American, the actions I have endeavored to outline here.

The self-appointed herdsmen and butchers of the global human-cattle ranch deny American exceptionalism, and their shills in media and government are trying to erase it from our consciousness. But it is very real.

The opening chapters of the Bible establish that human conscience, self-determination, and their natural consequences, are more important to the Creator of the universe even than His own plans – and in the New Testament, He proved, even more than His own life. The history of ancient Israel teaches as profoundly about the tendencies of fallen human government, and about our sinful addiction to it, as Locke, Bastiat, or Jefferson.

Christianity ignited the poetic Celtic soul of ancient England, gentled its Viking interlopers, and illuminated the English people's struggle with waves of invaders, and their equally-real struggles with generations of flawed kings who alternately protected, invaded, and plundered them.

America's spiritual forefathers, impelled equally by fervor for God and for the freedom He taught them, brought the lessons of all that history to these shores, embodied it all in our founding documents, principally our Declaration of Independence and Constitution. No other People in history has had the legal foundation of their social order based on the ultimate value of their individual lives and consciences; on their divinely-ordained right of self-determination before God and under His Law.

This recognition of God's Truth is the core of American exceptionalism, and the spring from which have flowed all the blessings we've enjoyed and shared with the world. Of course we are human, and fallen, and have used the power of our virtue to visit upon each other and upon the world, much of the evil that is in our hearts as well.

The prosperity and safety that virtue (and God's providence, and broad oceans) won, made us lazy and proud, as history teaches they always do. Some of us manifest those vices in passivity; others in unbounded avarice and worse passions. Thus we witness a marriage made in Hell; most of us facilitate with our money, safety, irresponsibility, and self-absorption, the hideous dreams of limitless, perverse indulgence and illusive ultimate power, of the wealthy, inhuman few.

The year of this writing, Anno Domini 2023, is the opening of a new era. In the first two decades this century, the satanic corruption long brewing in the corridors of power has been dragged out of the closet. Far from cringing in the light, it flaunts itself as Isaiah prophesied, *"...those who call evil good and good evil, who put darkness for light and light for darkness, who put bitter for sweet and sweet for bitter"*.

Comfort, cowardice, and dis-education long kept us passive in a pleasant illusion that the accelerating Hell-ward drift was a harmless and self-limiting oscillation of a pendulum. Now, the unprecedented criminal conspiracy that played out in our recent elections has made that illusion preposterous. Now, we must arrest and punish the perpetrators and make repetition of the crime impossible, or the recent theft of two elections and installation of an illegitimate president will guarantee that no political reversal of our Republic's diabolical implosion will ever again be possible.

Militia as enforcer of the Law with Grand Jury, the revitalization of which this book is intended to facilitate, is not just the only human structure that can meet this challenge, but *precisely the prescription of our inspired Founders, for this precise day, crime and emergency.*

I thank God for the long road He led me down, which culminated in writing this book. I pray that my efforts may be a small part of helping my countrymen to repent their dereliction and take up this sword, and that He will heal our land.

John Leyzorek
Elk Mountain
5 February, A.D. 2023

APPENDIX A

Constitution Enforcement & Militia Ordinance

This is Rev 27 of the version for the Commonwealth of Virginia. Please contact the author at securetheserights@protonmail.com for an editable text of the most current version, specific to your State.

An ORDINANCE SECURING THE U.S. CONSTITUTION and ESTABLISHING AND WELL-REGULATING MILITIA in the County/Municipality of_________________________________, in the Commonwealth of Virginia

[Short Title, "Constitution Enforcement and Militia

Ordinance"]

Preamble

We, the Board of Supervisors of _________________ COUNTY, *in the Commonwealth of Virginia, in pursuance of our oaths to uphold the Constitutions of our State and of the United States, and of our duty to our community under Divine Law, hereby establish our County as a Constitutional County, with the purpose of securing the fundamental and natural rights, powers, and authority of our Citizens, including but not limited to the right of self-defense, and defense of family and property, and hereby declare and exercise our right, authority and duty to restore and perpetually maintain the Constitutional Militia within this* [County, Parish or Borough], *for all purposes of Militia as stipulated by the People themselves in the United States Constitution.*

Article I. Justification

§1 WHEREAS, in the preamble to the Constitution for the United States, the American People declare that, "We The People...do ordain and establish this Constitution", thus clearly establishing that The People collectively occupy the highest sovereignty over all American government; and

§2 WHEREAS, the United States supreme Court in Chisolm v. Georgia, U.S. 2 Dall 419, 471 (1793), affirmed that, "The People are Sovereign...at the Revolution, the sovereignty devolved on the people; and they are truly the sovereigns of the country...equal as fellow citizens, and as joint tenants in the sovereignty"; and

*§3 WHEREAS, when the Declaration of Independence, recognized in American jurisprudence as Organic Law of this republic, recounting crimes of King George III, stated that, "He has dissolved Representative Houses repeatedly...whereby **the Legislative powers, incapable of Annihilation, have returned to the People at large for their exercise**", the American People collectively established that*

powers delegated by the People return to them, when the servant body to which they have been delegated abdicates, neglects, or refuses their proper exercise; and

§4 WHEREAS, the Virginia Resolution of 1798 states,"in case of a deliberate, palpable, and dangerous exercise of other powers, not granted by the [Constitution], the States who are parties thereto, have the right, and are in duty bound, to interpose for arresting the progress of the evil, and for maintaining within their respective limits, the authorities, rights and liberties appertaining to them"; and

§5 WHEREAS, the United States supreme Court in Printz v. United States, 521 U.S. 898 (1997), affirmed that, "The Constitution thus contemplates that a State's government will represent and remain accountable to its own Citizens" and quoting James Madison, "[T]he local or municipal authorities form distinct and independent portions of the supremacy, no more subject, within their respective spheres, to the general authority than the general authority is subject to them, within its own sphere" and further affirmed that, "This separation of the two spheres is one of the Constitution's structural protections of liberty"; and

§6 WHEREAS, in the same case, the United States supreme Court concluded, "The federal government may neither issue directives requiring the States to address particular problems, nor command the States' officers, or those of their political subdivisions, to administer or enforce a federal regulatory program...such commands are fundamentally incompatible with our constitutional system of dual sovereignty" – which, construing the subject clause of the Preamble of the Constitution in pari materia with its Tenth Amendment, applies to the county/state relationship as analogous to the state/federal; and

§7 WHEREAS, the Second Amendment of the United States Constitution reads "A well regulated Militia, being necessary to the security of a free State, the right of the people to keep and bear Arms, shall not be infringed"; and

§8 WHEREAS, the United States supreme Court in United States v. Miller, 307 U.S. 174 (1939), affirmed that firearms which are part of ordinary military equipment, or with uses that could contribute to the common defense, are protected by the Second Amendment; and

§9 WHEREAS, the United States supreme Court in District of Columbia v. Heller, 554 U.S. 570 (2008), affirmed the individual's right to possess firearms, unconnected with service in a militia, for traditionally lawful purposes such as self-defense within the home; and

§10 WHEREAS, the United States supreme Court in McDonald v. Chicago, 561 U.S. 742 (2010), affirmed that the right of an individual to "keep and bear arms," as protected under the Second Amendment, is incorporated by the Due Process Clause of the Fourteenth Amendment against the States; and

§11 WHEREAS, Article I, Section 13 of the Constitution of Virginia affirms, "That a well regulated militia, composed of the body of the people, trained to arms, is the proper, natural, and safe defense of a free state, therefore, the right of the people to keep and bear arms shall not be infringed;" and

§12 WHEREAS, certain legislation which has been or may be enacted by the legislature of this State, and which has been or may be enacted by the United States Congress, may infringe on the right, duty and authority of law-abiding Citizens to keep and bear arms to fulfill their duty stipulated in Article I, Section 8, Clause 15, and in the first clause of the Second Amendment, of the United States Constitution ; and

§13 WHEREAS, any 'red flag' 'ERPO' or similar process violates the Second, Fourth, Fifth, Sixth and Fourteenth Amendments of the U.S. Constitution and Sections 7, 8, 10, 11,13, and 15 of Article I of the Constitution of Virginia; and

§14 WHEREAS, the [Board, Commission] of
_______________________________ [County, Parish, Borough] believes that the legitimate and justifying role of government is to secure the

rights to life, liberty and property of the People as articulated in our Declaration of Independence; and

§15 Whereas, the Congress of the United States and the Governor and Legislature of Virginia have for too long utterly neglected their Constitutional duties in support of Militia; and

§16 WHEREAS, within its jurisdictional boundaries, this Board of Supervisors is willing to receive and properly exercise this delegated power and duty, incapable of Annihilation, from and on behalf of the People to whom it ultimately and originally belongs; and

§17 Whereas Art VI Sec 2 of the Constitution of the United States reads, " This Constitution, and the Laws of the United States which shall be made in Pursuance thereof;.... shall be the supreme Law of the Land;... any Thing in the Constitution or Laws of any State to the Contrary notwithstanding"; and

§18   Whereas Art VI Sec 3 of the Constitution of the United States reads, " all executive and judicial Officers, both of the United States and of the several States, shall be bound by Oath or Affirmation, to support this Constitution;...";

§19 IN ORDER to secure its Citizens' authority and duty to possess the means of self-defense and other unalienable rights, and to execute the necessary, essential,and indispensable duty to organize and regulate Militia for the same and related purposes as well as for its Constitutional duties, and to honor its oath to uphold the Constitutions of this State and of the United States and the supremacy thereof,

Article II. Ordered

§1 NOW, THEREFORE, BE IT RESOLVED, that the [Board, Commission,] *of* ___________________________ [County, Parish or Borough] *hereby expresses its intent to perform within our jurisdiction the abdicated duties required of the State and of the Congress as stipulated by We The People in Article I, Section 8,*

Clauses 15 and 16 and in the Second Amendment to the Constitution of the United States, and our intent to oppose by all lawful means any order or enactment that may unconstitutionally infringe the rights of its Citizens; and that

§2 The [Board, Commission] *of* ________________________________
[County, Parish or Borough] *hereby ORDERS that NO public funds under its control, nor time of employees, nor physical property and equipment of the* [County, Parish or Borough] *may be used to restrict or infringe rights protected by the Constitution of the United States, including the Second Amendment rights of our Citizens, or to aid or cooperate with federal, state, or other agencies in any such restriction or infringement of said rights; any County employee cooperating in such infringement being subject to dismissal; and that*

§3 The Board of Supervisors of ________________________________ *County hereby ORDERS that its human and material resources SHALL be applied as necessary to oppose, resist, obstruct, and interpose to the maximum practical degree against any infringement on the authority and duty of its Citizens, including the authority and duty to keep and bear arms in Militia and the right to keep and bear arms for personal and home defense, using such legal means as are recognized and expedient to deter, prevent and obstruct any other crime, including but not limited to court action, with failure of any County employee to do so within the scope of her/his employment being grounds for dismissal; and that*

§4 Searches and Seizures of Firearms and other Militia Accoutrements Under 'Red Flag' Laws.

To secure the guaranteed due process and other rights of County residents, NO search for or seizure of a citizen's firearms, ammunition, Militia accoutrements and/or related personal property, under any 'red flag', 'ERPO' or similar purported law, enactment, or regulation shall be allowed to proceed in the County. Any complaint, application, or process intended to result in such an order or action, shall be immediately transmitted to the Grand Jury for investigation of all parties and witnesses named or participating therein. If no Grand

Jury is sitting, one shall immediately be impaneled for the purpose, and the information transmitted thereto; and that

§5 The [Board, Commission,] *of* _________________________
[County, Parish or Borough] *hereby establishes that it shall be an offense to make a complaint under any "red flag", "ERPO" or similar law or purported law alleging a danger that cannot be proven beyond reasonable doubt to exist, with each such offense punishable by a fine of no less than $1,000 or one year in jail, or both. If any trespass or seizure has taken place as a result of such unprovable complaint, in addition to the specified fine or imprisonment, the individual or entity that filed the complaint leading to the 'red flag' action ('Complainant') shall within 30 days of notice pay to the Court its stipulated reimbursement to Target for all costs arising from the Action ('Damages'), including but not limited to a) Target's demonstrated loss of earnings; b) All of Target's property seized and not restored in like condition to that in which it was seized in the Action; c) any other damage to any of Target's property; and d) Attorneys' fees, court costs and all other costs demonstrably arising from the Action. If Complainant fails to pay the Damages within 60 days from date of notice by the Court, Damages are hereby statutorily tripled and the County Militia shall seize, in* ex parte *action, all such property of Complainant as required to satisfy the Court's stipulated Damages payable to Target; and that*

§6 The [Board, Commission] *of*
_________________________________ [County, Parish, Borough]
hereby establishes its Constitutional Militia, to include all County Citizens without felony records or history of adjudicated mental incompetence, who are willing and able to aid in defending this community and upholding the Law; and that

§7 The [Board, Commission] *of* _____________________
[County, Parish or Borough] *shall provide in the most timely way possible and in no case later than sixty (60) days from the date hereof, for the necessary staffing and public funding to restore the Militia in this County, during any and all such periods as the State*

Legislature shall continue in abdication and/or violation of duty as stipulated in Article I, Section 8, Clause 16 of the Constitution for the United States; and that

§8 The [Board, Commission] *of* ________________________ [County, Parish or Borough] *shall administer and well regulate its County Militia as follows:*

1. Nomination and Appointment of Officers.

This Body shall promptly appoint officers nominated by their respective units and according to a uniform command structure mutually agreed on by all units in the County. Said power of appointment of officers shall revert to the State Governor during all such times as the State Legislature has ceased its abdication or avoidance of its constitutional duty for the same.

No nominee may have been convicted of a felony in any State, or may have been adjudicated mentally incompetent, or be regularly taking any drugs proven to cause mental impairment, and all officers must take an oath to uphold, defend, and enforce the Constitutions of this State and of the United States and all laws made in pursuance thereof, before entering upon their official duties.

2. County Militia Liaison and Coordination.

All units of County Militia must choose and report one officer from among all of them to serve as County Militia Liaison Officer, and one to serve in the incapacity of the first. Duties of the County Militia Liaison Officer shall be to coordinate operations among the several units, to coordinate operations with Militias of other jurisdictions and with paid law enforcement agencies, and to coordinate with the State at all times during which the State is performing its duties for constitutional Militia as stipulated by the People in the Constitution.

The County Militia Liaison Officer shall report to this Board/Commission on all Militia activities within the County and involving County Militia units, when requested by this Board/Commission.

3. Minimum Standards of Mental and Physical Fitness.

Uniform minimum standards of mental and physical fitness shall be adopted and updated as necessary by all militia units in the County; shall include no history of any adjudication of mental incompetence, no use of drugs proven to cause mental impairment, and the taking of an oath to uphold defend and enforce the Constitutions of this State and of the United States and all laws made in pursuance thereof, prior to the individual entering upon official duties, and shall be reported to this Board/Commission.

4. Arms, Ammunition and Accoutrements.

Citizens shall provide their own firearms, ammunition and tactical accoutrements, meeting uniform standards adopted by all County Militia units, and keep them in good repair. However, as funds allow, the County may provide ammunition and other equipment.

5. County Militia Training.

A uniform, minimum mandatory training program and schedule for new recruits and for existing members shall be adopted and updated as necessary by all County Militia units, and shall be reported to this Board/Commission.

6. Coordination and Cooperation With Paid Public Peace Officers.

All County Militia units shall cooperate and coordinate with existing paid municipal, County, and State public peace officers, upon the official request of these agencies, made through the County Militia Liaison Officer.

However, County Militia shall be responsible to the Citizens of the County and to the Constitutions of this State and of the United States, and shall NOT cooperate in, or permit, the enforcement of any enactment or supposed law which is null by reason of its conflict with the natural rights of Citizens or with the Constitutions of this State or of the United States. In <u>Marbury v. Madison (1803)</u> the U.S. Supreme Court affirmed that "(a) Law repugnant to the Constitution is void."

7. Minimum Standards of Personal Grooming and Respectful Public Behavior.

Uniform minimum standards of personal grooming and respectful public behavior for Militia members shall be adopted and updated as necessary by all militia units in the County, to protect the effectiveness of members and promote public confidence in our Militia. Excessive or inappropriate use of coarse language and display of symbols associated with death, lawlessness, rebellion, or wanton violence shall not be permitted.

8. Law Enforcement Duty Coordinated With and Directed by Grand Jury.

Especially in cases in which one or more members of paid public law enforcement or other public officials are being investigated by the Grand Jury, law enforcement duty including but not limited to collection of evidence and service of search and arrest warrants, shall be a core function of this Militia, as coordinated with, and directed by, the Grand Jury of this [County, Parish or Borough].

9. Grand Jury Anonymity.

Uniform protocols shall be adopted by all County Militia units to protect and preserve anonymity of subjects of investigation and of members of the Grand Jury, particularly in investigations of public officials or paid law enforcement personnel or agencies.

10. Removals for Cause.

Violation by any Militia member or officer of his or her Oath to defend and enforce the Constitutions of this State and of the United States and all laws made in pursuance thereof, shall be punishable by removal from membership or office.

11 Transparency and coordination

The County shall make a page available on its web-site if any, or prominently post there a link, for the County Militia's use to present its organization, activities, membership standards and application, and to solicit contact.

12 Regulation

In the event that a Militia unit fails to abide by the procedures adopted hereunder and its effectiveness or availability for its necessary Constitutional functions is thereby impaired, this body may withdraw recognition of the unit, may direct the nomination of new officers to replace some or all of those formerly approved, or may direct that it be disbanded and re-formed, taking care that the corrections proceed with such expedition as may be required to assure availability of militia for its necessary Constitutional functions.

13. SEVERABILITY *If any section, part or provision of this Ordinance is declared unconstitutional or invalid by a court of competent jurisdiction, then it is expressly provided and it is the intention of the [name of county board or commission] in passing this Ordinance that its parts shall be severable and all other parts of this Ordinance shall not be affected thereby and they shall remain in full force and effect.*

14. EFFECTIVE DATE. *This Ordinance shall take effect immediately upon its passage.*

ORDAINED *by the Board of Supervisors of_____________COUNTY, Virginia, this_____Day of [month] in the Year of our Lord 20____*

____

[Supervisor]

____

[Supervisor]

[Supervisor]

MODCOMILORD rev 27 VA

APPENDIX B
Model By-Laws

Draft By-Laws for _____________ County Militia

Rev 12 by John Leyzorek

Article I Name, Definition and Purpose:

§ 1 The organization shall be _____________ Militias, and it shall be a Militia, defined as follows:

1 As the collective expression of the God-given unalienable rights, and indefeasible duties, of individual and community self-defense

2 By George Mason as, "the whole people, except for a few public officials".

3 By its duties under our Constitution to "execute the Laws of the Union, suppress Insurrections and repel Invasions"

4 By its character under our Constitution as

75

"necessary to the security of a free State"

§ 2 The purposes of the organization shall be limited to

1 protecting all peaceful citizens and residents of [STATE] and of others of the United States against real or imminent physical threats of any and all kinds, natural and man-made, and against usurpations and abridgements of their natural and of their Constitutionally-protected rights, especially but not limited to the right of individual and community self-defense. This section includes the Constitutionally-mandated duties of suppression of insurrections and repulsion of invasions.

2 Enforcing the Constitutions of [STATE} and of the United States and all laws made in pursuance thereof, and the enumerated natural rights secured therein, and other non-enumerated natural rights, with particular attention to violations of rights under color of law; and in close cooperation with the Grand Jury. This section includes the Constitutionally-mandated duty of executing the Laws of the Union.

3 This is not a prepper club or self-protection society. We recognize our responsibility to the entirety of our community, to our State, and to our Republic.

§ 3 This organization shall not support or advocate for any candidate or ballot issue.

§ 4 This organization recognizes only one Human Race, including vast variety of appearance and character, each member endowed by his or her Creator with the same inalienable rights.

§ 5 To enhance its ability to serve the community by multiplying resources, and increasing capacity and geographic reach, this organization shall work diligently to integrate its functional and command structure with those of other groups with compatible goals in the County and region, but shall not compromise the values and principles set forth herein.

Article II Jurisdiction:

§1   Area of operation and jurisdiction shall be [COUNTY, STATE]. The Militia may operate outside __________ County if any one or more of the following conditions is satisfied

1 Operation outside the County is an essential and urgent part of dealing with a County issue. Coordination with local authorities should always be sought.

2 The Militia's assistance is officially requested by a legitimate similar unit, or other legitimate law-enforcement agency, and the Militia can respond to the request without compromising its local obligations

3 The Militia is called into State service according to Law and for lawful purposes, and the Militia can respond to the request without compromising its local obligations,

4 The Militia is called into federal service according to Law and for lawful purposes, and the Militia can respond to the request without compromising its local obligations; however under no circumstances may federal service involve service outside the territorial limits of the United States.

Article III Membership

§1 Membership shall be open to any citizen or legal resident of this State or of the United States, residing in or having ties to _________ County; who is not a paid official or employee with executive or supervisory responsibility of any government; who has not been convicted of a felony in any State; whose character and principles have satisfactorily passed investigation, and who will swear the following oath:

Freely and knowingly I do solemnly swear to uphold and defend the God-given rights of all men, the Constitutions of [STATE] and of the united States, and the lives and property of all peaceful men, against all enemies foreign or domestic; to these ends I will obey the By-Laws of this Militia, and the lawful orders of those placed lawfully in authority over me according to said By-Laws , and I will obey no unlawful orders. To the support of this oath I pledge my life, my fortune, and my sacred honor, so help me God.

§ 2 Moslems are ineligible to membership in this organization because their belief system supersedes our Constitution and renders any oath they may swear valueless. Members of other secret societies may be similarly ineligible if there is reason to question their loyalty to the Constitution or the sincerity of their oath.

Former Moslems or former members of such societies may apply for membership if they make a credible public renunciation of that faith or affiliation.

§ 3 Applicants for membership shall be vetted to assure that they will be assets to the Militia and community in that role. Information about their character may be gathered from any source, including Internet postings, publications, employers,   neighbors and acquaintances, however their privacy will not be compromisd by public disclosure of any information gathered. Evidence of a relish for violence; of intent to act, or advocate for acting, on racial prejudice; or of disrespect for due process and rule of law, shall tend to disqualify an applicant.

§ 4 Membership shall not be limited by age, sex, or ability; however no member under the age of 18 shall be eligible for hazardous duty except under extraordinary necessity, and all members must be judged fit for their assigned duties by their commanding officers, and must make timely disclosure to same of any relevant disabilities.

§ 5 "Men" in this document shall refer to all humans, regardless of age or sex.

§ 6 No member may be an habitual user of any drug or substance, legal or otherwise, that impairs his effective functioning or judgement, nor may any member report for duty under such influence. Violation of this requirement is grounds for dismissal.

§ 7 Refusal of a lawful order is grounds for dismissal.

§ 8 Members must cooperate with appropriate skills training, physical training and conditioning exercises and requirements, to support their effectiveness. Persistent failure to do so is grounds for dismissal.

§ 9 By accepting these By-Laws all members affirm that they understand that militia duty and training is inherently hazardous. Every member commits to work diligently to minimize and mitigate hazards, to other members and to the public, therefore every member is responsible to observe and appropriately alert other members to any hazardous conduct occurring during training. Every member affirms that he takes on these unavoidable hazards willingly and knowingly, and that any injuries to himself or damage to his property are his responsibility alone.

§ 10 Members must conduct themselves at all times in a peaceful, responsible, gentle manner and diligently refrain from engaging in conduct unnecessarily threatening, demeaning or degrading to anyone. We are the People, the conscience of the People, and the defenders of the People's Law safety and civilization. We cannot function without the confidence of the People/our neighbors, and we must never undermine it. Conduct damaging to the reputation or mission of the Militia is grounds for dismissal

§11. Membership requires participation. The Militia also needs friends and allies and any person may be a Friend of __________

County Militia, but shall not be a Member, shall not vote, and shall not receive information about or participate in operations unless he has attended 50% of general meetings and appropriate training events since joining.

§12 No member may make any statement on behalf of the Militia, or participate in any public activity in the character of a Member of the Militia, without explicit authorization by the Guidance Committee. Our effectiveness depends on our reputation.

Participation in questionable activities or making questionable statements, even if the member insists that he is acting on his own without the authority of the group, still reflects on this Militia and on all Militia.

Article IV Decision-Making and Command Structure

§ 1 Governance

Para 1 The Militia has a dual system of governance. General functioning of the group, including application of membership standards, member admission and expulsion; and execution of decisions about by-laws, plans, and actions to engage in, will be overseen by the Guidance Committee, which shall consist of a Chairman; the Intelligence Officer, the Liaison and Communications Officer, the Public Information and Relations Officer, the Logistics and Supply Officer, Membership Officer, Training Officer, and the Operational Commander. As membership constraints require and qualifications allow, one individual may hold multiple titles/responsibilities, however concentration of responsibility should be minimized., to bring the widest possible perspective and knowledge base to the guidance function.

Para 2 Appointment and duties of Guidance Committee Members

All Guidance Committee members shall be elected from among the membership, and may be removed, by ¾ majority of members present at a meeting announced for the purpose two weeks ahead of time. In an emergency, the Committee may remove one of its members by consensus, however the removal is subject to review by the membership ASAP.

Each Committee Member shall appoint an assistant to help him and replace him in his unavoidable temporary absence.

Para 3 Duties of Guidance Committee Members

Chairman Duties shall include assuring the orderly progress of meetings and keeping of Minutes (for which purpose he may appoint a Secretary), calling meetings in response to events or concerns raised by Members (if two or more members request a meeting on a given subject, it shall be scheduled and held within two weeks), and participation in the Committee's deliberations.

Intelligence Officer shall be responsible for designing, organizing, and directing the intelligence-gathering functions of the Militia. Information that must be gathered and kept current includes belief systems and probable intentions of any significant actors in the AO, movements ongoing and planned of any groups or forces relevant to the community, intentions of outside groups including government entities, criminal elements, refugees, gangs, etc, that may at any point impinge on the safety, resources, and rights of the community, and current and future disposition and availability of resources necessary to the health of the community and operations of the Militia.. Appropriate intelligence sharing with other groups is a core function.

Liaison and Communications Officer Duties shall include all necessary official communication with government bodies, other Militia groups, paid law-enforcement agencies; all membership notifications and callouts; and specifying, recommending training in, and oversight of all operational communications equipment and methods for the Militia. He may appoint a technical specialist if needed.

Public Information/Relations Officer Duties shall include all necessary authorized official communication with the public, including news media, and advising Guidance Committee on the Militia's standing in the community, how proposed actions may affect it, and how to improve it. No public statements shall be made nor information released, and no questions may be answered for non-Members, except as specifically authorized by the Guidance Committee.

Logistics/Supply Officer Duties shall include planning and oversight of all movements of personnel and equipment of the

Militia; and planning, inventory maintenance, and acquisition and protection of all supplies and equipment, including but not limited to food, water, weapons and ammunition, vehicles, fuels, medical supplies and equipment, and other materiel belonging to or used by the Militia. His input is essential to judging feasibility of all actions of the Militia during the planning process, and to supporting them in the field.

Membership Officer duties shall include recruiting and vetting new members, informing the Committee of special needs of all and of individual members, maintaining membership lists which shall include record of date of admission and oath, contact information, availability, and level of health, skills and training of each member; and maintaining the security of such lists. Membership list shall be available only to the Guidance Committee.

Training Officer duties shall include scheduling and providing (in the dereliction of the State) for all training prescribed by Congress and/or by the Guidance Committee, developing training program in Congress's dereliction for adoption by Guidance Committee, and seeking out sources for useful training of all types to suggest to the Guidance Committee.

Operational Commander or his designee shall command all external operations of the Militia of all kinds, and shall be ultimately responsible for the highest possible level of personnel and public safety and for the successful completion of the operation. All military, quasi-military, law-enforcement, and training operations shall be under the exclusive command of the Operations Commander and his subordinates. Operational Commander shall devise and maintain his subordinate command stucture, subject to the approval of the Guidance Committee.

§ 2   Meetings, Voting, and Responsibility

Para 1 Decisions about by-laws, plans, and actions to engage in shall be made by ¾ majority vote of members present at a meeting announced for the purpose two weeks in advance, however emergency action decisions may be made by the Guidance Committee alone, subject to review by the Members at the earliest possible date. Decisions about admission, expulsion, or discipline of a member shall be made by the Guidance Committee.

Para 2 Minutes must be kept for all meetings of the membership and of the Guidance Committee, and shall record members present, major points of discussion, decisions made, shall be approved by those present before adjournment of each meeting, and shall be available on request to any Member, but shall not be distributed outside the Militia.

Para 3   Militiamen are volunteers, and may refuse to participate in a specific action if they have personal beliefs or responsibilities that interfere. However a consistent pattern of refusal may be grounds for dismissal. Once a member accepts an assignment, he is bound to obey the orders of the officer in charge.

§3 Operational ranks, duties, qualifications

1 Operational Commander shall nominate and Members shall approve by ¾ majority all subordinate officers and assignments of rank.

§4 Resignations, removals, and replacement of officers

Para 1 Guidance Commitee members who resign, die, or are removed shall be replaced by election from the membership at the next scheduled membership meeting, replacement to be announced as an agenda item two weeks before the meeting. If required by exigent circumstances a temporary replacement may be made by the remainder of the Guidance Committee to serve until the next meeting of the Membership.

Para 2 A Guidance Committee member may be removed by vote of ¾ of the members present at a meeting announced for the purpose 2 weeks in advance. Such a meeting must be scheduled on motion of 1/3 of the Membership delivered to the Committee, or presented at a Membership Meeting.

Para 3 If exigent curcumstances require, a Guidance Committee member may be removed by unanimous consensus of the remaining Committee, subject to approval by ¾ majority at the next Membership Meeting.

Para 4 Any operational officer or member may be removed or demoted for cause at any time by his superior officer, however removals must be investigated, reviewed, and approved or reversed at the earliest practical date by the Guidance Committee.

Para 5 Any Officer may be relieved of duty by one or more of his subordinates, but not by his immediate subordinate, at any time, but only for the gravest causes, such as the giving of unlawful orders, unjustified order to surrender, insanity, or treason. However any such reliefs or removals shall be investigated as possible insubordination or treason, at the earliest practical date, by the Guidance Committee. A removed or relieved officer shall be replaced by his immediate subordinate, subject to review at the earliest practical date by the Guidance Committee.

Article V Rules of Engagement

§1 Natural Law and all valid civil laws must be followed by all members at all times, unless doing so creates a reasonable danger of immediate harm to the member, or seriously impedes an urgent, necessary, and lawful mission.

§2 All persons, animals, and property must be treated with respect at all times, unless they pose an immediate danger to a member or to the lawful mission, in which case the minimum force required to mitigate the danger must be used.

§3 Women and children are to be treated as non-combatants and shown all possible courtesy at all times, unless they present a clear danger or are engaged in deliberate hostile activity, in which case the minimum of force needed to mitigate the danger shall be used.

§4 No non-combatant shall be deprived of presumption of innocence, fair trial, or other natural or Constitutionally-protected right.

§5 In all cases possible and consistent with its lawful mission, Militia activity shall be coordinated with, and at the request of, the appropriate agencies of established lawful government, including paid police agencies and the Grand Jury.

Article VI Communication

§1 Communication about activities, membership, and equipment of the organization shall take place only among members and only as necessary or ordered to support operations

§2 No member may make any public statement on behalf of the organization without specific authorization

§3 All members must monitor designated channels of communication as ordered, to assure timely response

§4 Effective means for timely communication within the Militia and with similar groups outside the AO must be established and maintained independent of any non-Militia-controlled infrastructure.

Article VII Adoption and Amendment

§1 These by-laws must be adopted, and may be amended,

by ¾ of all members present in person at a meeting for which two weeks notice has been given.

APPENDIX C
Answers to Questions

"My State Code (Texas) prohibits Militia"

Okay, a general answer and a specific. The general answer is that Militia is described as 'necessary' in the Constitution. Any law repugnant to the Constitution is void. Therefore any law prohibiting militia is not law, unenforceable, has no legal existence. That is the best ground to stand on.

Specifically, the Texas statute reads, *"Except as provided by Subsection (b), a body of persons other than the regularly organized Texas military forces, the armed forces of the United States, or the active militia of another state may not associate as a military company or organization or parade in public with firearms in a municipality of the state."*

If accused of violating this statute, I could also argue, "I am not a 'military company' or part thereof. Militia is not 'military'; Militia refers to all citizens able to participate in defense of their community, whereas 'military' refers to paid soldiery, under continuous central command, and distinct from the citizenry.

But the second argument relies on mincing words, whereas the first stands firm on the bedrock of the Constitution.

Will this approach "work" in court? God knows! Even a lawyer, which this writer is not, cannot predict that. What we all know is that the system....all the "systems" tend to be rigged in favor of the power structure. But the entire campaign this book is written to support, is about re-structuring the power, to the way our Founders intended, and many fought and died, to structure it. That is with we-the-people, by and for whom the structure is built, at the top.

Your homework, the degree to which your unit earns the trust, support, and love of your community; the degree to which it has earned the confidence and respect of paid law-enforcement, the legal standing you achieved by passage of the Constitution Enforcement and Militia Ordinance and the companion Grand Jury Ordinance; your level of tactical capability; and the strength and reach of your network with other similar groups, will determine the outcome of "legal" challenges, just as much as words on paper or parchment.

In 1776 we set forth some pretty radical "legal" principles. Although they had good precedent not only in Scripture but in the English Common Law, most of the lawsters and judges would have said they were treasonable nonsense. But by 1783, we had established them as law, by force of arms.

I do not expect and do not advocate that armed conflict will be needed to re-establish the principles of our Declaration of Independence. As long as we do our diligence in community relations, education, public relations, and *capability*, we should be able to consider that work was done once for all..

As for what I mean by *capability*, when a police officer pulls you over for a burnt-out taillight, neither you nor he expects that the pistol on his hip will be used. But its presence does influence your conversation. It make it much more likely that you will accept the officer's interpretation of the law, and peacefully sign the ticket.

Our Founders wrote that militia is necessary to the security of a free State, and they acknowledged its authority to execute the Law. Noah Webster wrote in 1787, " The supreme power in America cannot enforce unjust laws by the sword; because the whole body of the people are armed, and constitute a force superior to any band of regular troops that can be, on any pretence, raised in the United States." These facts and statements recognize not exactly that force makes law, but that law stands only when enforced. And as we see today in our mostly-peaceful society, "enforcement" usually does not mean *use* of force, but *availability of force*. That is the element that must be brought to the restoration of our Republic, by *Militia. The formula will work, if we follow it.*

APPENDIX D

"County Handout (Revision 13)",
Rollout Critical Path,
And a Fuller Discussion

We The People ordained government to secure our rights, not trample them. Americans want to end the criminality that has taken over our governments, State and federal: fake virus hysteria justifying lawless lockdown, gun grabs and 'red flags', Islamic jihad by stealth, fake elections, and more.

The plan developed by TACTICAL CIVICS™ is the only lawful, peaceful, practical, comprehensive way to stop our rogue servants who violate the Constitution with impunity, and to bring freedom roaring back. Freedom and common sense can be enforced, starting in your County. This is not politics, but a new way of life.

LOCAL ACTION SEQUENCE for Constitution Enforcement

1) Plant your TACTICAL CIVICS™ County Chapter, or similar Constitution education and advocacy group. Just a handful of committed folks is enough, but this is action, not just more talk-talk

2) Find or start a respectable, community-oriented militia group in your county who will commit to the process of earning Constitutional standing by County Ordinance. The militia group prepares its list of officers for appointment, and membership standards and training protocols for adoption at the County governing body meeting when our Constitution Enforcement and Militia Ordinance, and grand Jury Ordinance, are passed.

3) Get your local sheriff on board if you can (like judges, sheriffs are politicians first, no matter how good their speeches sound). Militia is the Constitution's only stipulated law enforcement; it is controlled by and comprised of the People themselves. To honor his oath, your sheriff is required to support Grand Jury and Constitutional Militia, which can be his most effective partner, or his biggest political nightmare.

4) Recruit gun shop owners, tactical trainers, shooting ranges, out-fitters, and any other willing businesses in your county to become Affiliates of your Militia or of your Constitution advocacy club. These relationships can provide rallying places, links with the business community (county governments listen to business), and first choice for purchasing Militia arms and equipment.

5) Raise enough committed citizens in your county who will show up to pack the County governing body meeting.

6) Present our Ordinances to one or more of your county government members (www.securetheserights.net, or the Tactical Civics organization can provide the pitch, and the Ordinances, customizable for your State) and get it on the Agenda.

7) Pack the County meeting. Have video, media, and bloggers there, and get the Ordinances passed. As soon as the Ordinances are passed, at that meeting present officers for appointment and procedures for approval, as specified in the Ordinance. Hold Militia sign-up right there. Announce your first official training and recruitment day.

8) Have your advocacy group file press releases with media in your county, on your groups' pages online, and with bloggers in the area, explaining what The People are doing. www.securetheserights.net can help draft the texts.

Background

Militia is the only thing defined as 'necessary' in the Constitution, and the only law enforcement recognized in that Law, so nobody can tell you that it cannot meet. If authorities are trying to impose restrictions on meeting, use common sense, of course; your Militia may wish to consult with local doctors and other knowledgeable people to decide what responses to the virus, or other threats, will and will not be made in your county.

Militia is the highest law-enforcement body in your county, but it need not replace nor conflict with the work that paid police agencies do, and they should be offered its support and cooperation. But Militia's first responsibility is to the Constitution and its community. It can also pursue certain threats and crimes that paid agencies can't or won't (corrupt officials, gangs, jihadis).

The Other Missing Piece of Law Enforcement

Grand Jury, the other pre-Constitutional Law Enforcement in our system, is Militia's essential partner.

TACTICAL CIVICS™ or www.securetheserights.net can provide materials to educate the jury pool, or a sitting Grand Jury, about its powers. If you know of or suspect serious ongoing crime in your area, petition your county court to seat a Grand Jury (or other specific procedure for your State). Notify local media. Give the court (7) days to comply.

If the judge refuses, make your county sheriff seat the Grand Jury; a sheriff's duty when a court refuses.

As long as it remains in session, the Grand Jury has full use of the courthouse. If necessary, have your Militia unit and sheriff enforce this basic rule of law. You can deliver to the Grand Jury via county clerk the TACTICAL CIVICS™ Vol. 2 Field Handbook, *Grand Jury Awake*, and any felony presentments.

Your recognized Constitutional Militia can also offer your County:

- Church, school, business, and event Security Teams and training

- Anti-Jihad training and defense

- A new, healthy, community-building social outlet for all ages, including at-risk youth

Equal publicity must go to the Constitutional advocacy group, the local Militia unit, and any participating paid law enforcement units. We must re-train the American mind; We The People now begin restoring rule of law by serving in America's two ancient law enforcement institutions. Your county can show neighboring counties and the rest of our Republic what is possible.

TACTICAL CIVICS™ NATIONAL PLAN

TC seeks to plant county chapters in all 3141counties in America; a unified network of citizens who know civics and have a detailed tactical plan to enforce the Constitution and defend their communities against all threats including lawless public servants. TC's website contains videos, podcasts, blog articles, and free eBooks, as does www.securetheserights.net Enforcing our Constitution as its writers intended must be our new way of life, including continuous training, supporting and organizing of our fellowAmericans to restore and preserve freedom by self-responsibility

1) Restore Militia in every county and jointly deploy them with well-briefed Grand Juries: violating the Constitution will no longer be the crime every official gets away with;

2) Finish ratifying the First Right in our Bill of Rights, breaking the U.S. House into small districts that ordinary Americans can afford to run for and serve in;

3) Bring Congress Home; the world's first distributed legislature,

now under our watchful eye;

4) Deploy TC's Indictment Engine™ to track and arrest legislation that violates the Constitution;

5) Through TC's 19 Reform Laws, over time we scrape back all we've lost to DC organized crime.

NOW...IT'S YOUR MOVE!   Go to https://TacticalCivics.com or www.securetheserights.net   TC Handout Rev 13

Fuller Discussion

All the 'bad stuff' that we see our government servants doing, or fear that they are about to do, whether it is lockdowns, counterfeit money, invasions on gun and other property rights, jerking us around in a corrupt court system, all these things are simply crimes. If I did them to you, I'd go to jail. But a guy we pay to do some government chores, gets away with a whole career of it, then we pay him a fat retirement.

Why? Because we have forgotten that We The People built our government to secure our rights, that we and only we own, and are sovereign over it all. And for the whole existence of our Republic we have neglected our Constitutional duty to enforce the Law. Instead we have given that duty and power over to 'professionals', who are part of the government: Of course they will not arrest their co-workers or bosses, who sign their paychecks.

So here is the process we need to follow to get back into our proper Constitutional position of power over the servants. Just like a military operation, all the parts have to be right, and done in the right order, by the right guys. Haste, carelessness, ego, skipping steps, overconfidence lead to failure.

First, a Militia group. It needs to be well-organized around its constitutional   duties   and   community   role. www.securetheserights.net can provide a set of by-laws that cover

97

all the bases, if you do not already, or need an upgrade. It needs to have a credible membership. Three guys, plus four others who never show up, is not good. It needs to have a real training program. Firearms stuff is good, but just as necessary are first aid, disaster response, rescue operations, land navigation, crowd control, evidence handling...

Second, the group needs to look good. This is not BS. The group needs the support of the community: if it does not have that support and confidence, who will nurse wounded, bring hot coffee to night patrollers, misdirect the invaders, reload ammo, donate blankets, cook food, monitor radios? And who will come to the county government meeting and tell the commissioners *"Yes, these are the GOOD GUYS and we need you to pass this ordinance recognizing and empowering their vital role in our community!"?*

The group needs to look good so that the County governing body members (who are after all politicians) will not have to worry about political fallout from passing our Ordinance ("What? You passed an Ordinance for *that* bunch of lowlifes!?"). You may need to take longtime members who have criminal records, unusually wild tattoos, or who have really pissed off the commission in the past, off your membership roster, to make your group look better.

You don't like that? Nobody likes to get shot at, but we are prepared to do it, for the defense of our community. We must be willing to take other kinds of pain, too, and swallow our pride if it's the price of victory. We must be willing to be cagey, and recognize political reality, in the great cause of restoring our Republic, rule of law, and the freedom and security of our homes and families. There will be plenty of roles for good guys who ain't pretty, out of the spotlight.

Part of looking good is earning the trust and gratitude of the community. Helping the homeless, bringing firewood to the widow, cutting fallen trees out of the road, picking up trash, operating food banks, finding lost dogs, fixing the roof for the family that lost employment, guarding the business with the broken window, trapping the coon that is stealing the cat-food... *any* need in your community can be an opportunity to do your personal duty as a good Samaritan, and earn the trust of your neighbors.

Third, make allies. There must be a TACTICAL CIVICS™ Chapter or similar Constitution advocacy group in your county. This will be the hub for education of your whole community in true American civics, in the importance of Militia, and for education of Grand Juries, which will be Militia's essential partner in their law-enforcement duties. The Chapter, and the militia, must recruit local businesses to be Affiliates. Gun shops and tactical trainers are naturals, and can drum up business in the process by offering meeting space, copying, etc., to the group and providing gear or training at a discount. But any business can earn itself goodwill by publicly backing the Good Guys, and make a powerful statement in favor of the Ordinance at the county governing body meeting. Local government listens to local business.

You should approach your sheriff and chief of police, if you have reason to believe they are true supporters of the Constitution, and reasonable people. Although your Militia has primary constitutional authority and they do not, they are important, accepted parts of the community and should not fear that you are trying to replace them. They know many parts of the job that you do not. But you can offer them huge supplementary manpower and firepower, and probably other skills, and information. You can also tackle problems that are politically too hot for them to handle. You and they should already be mutually known and trusted from your group's community service work. Their voices at the county meeting in favor of our Ordinance will be very powerful. If they will not back you as you offer to back them, perhaps they have something to hide.

Fourth, approach members of your county governing body. As members of the community, you are their bosses, and you have a proposal to improve the safety and security of the community, to secure everyone's rights, to fight crime more effectively than was thought possible. In fact, recognizing and supporting Militia is the constitutional duty of government. Give this job to your most articulate member. Do not use a public meeting for the first approach, where the commissioner will be more conscious of how he looks than of what you are saying. Tackle only the ones you think will be receptive to the idea, or who are noisy about their support for the Constitution. Do not try to get them together, because secret meetings are illegal in most states, and, again, together they will be thinking politics rather than listening to you.

You are not begging. You're the boss, and this is their duty. Still, there is nothing gained by being disrespectful or nasty. Be clear and definite. It will do no harm to point out that it will be a good thing for them politically, to be on the side of bringing new security and protecting freedom in the county.

Fifth, with your allies on the board or commission, plan and schedule the meeting. Take care to follow legal requirements for public notice and agenda. Make sure the agenda item covers not only the Ordinances themselves but signup, appointments, and approvals. Your governing body cannot legally act on anything that is not on the agenda. **Make sure all your supporters will turn out** and pack the meeting room. Make sure your Militia members are also there in force, but not conspicuously or illegally armed, or in a threatening mood. Do not give your commissioners or the public any excuse for backpedaling or cold feet. Make sure your members are ready to formally sign up, and have your lists of officers and procedures ready for appointment and approval.

Make sure you have your best spokesman there, and make sure he or she is studied-up to answer any question or objection that may be raised. Www.securetheserights.net can provide study materials, and answer specific questions, but we can't attend the meeting. After all, we do not live in your county and it would not look good for outsiders to be speaking for you, but we can porovide a speech that can be used to introduce the Ordinance.

Sixth, Meeting! Pack the room with your members and supporters. Let your ally on the board introduce the Ordinance. He can give the speech, or you can. During the discussion, answer any questions clearly and firmly. All you're asking for is what the Law demands and your community needs. Cheer your commission when they pass it! Move immediately to the sign up, and approval/appointment of officers and procedures. Don't allow time for second thoughts or foot-dragging.

And on the **seventh** day, rest! Yes, we're hot to start taking down the criminals. But if you're the first county to pass the Ordinance and have fully constitutional Militia, you should continue building your good reputation with community service, preparedness education, and helping the paid law enforcement while you **wait** for a few surrounding counties to pass the Ordinance; the word will travel fast.

The first time you try to take down a powerful crook, you *will* encounter resistance... maybe physical, certainly procedural, as the other crooks in the system back their buddy up with all kinds of obstruction tactics. You must have backup, in the form of public awareness and support beyond your own county; in the form of other similar simultaneous actions, in the form of other Militias and Grand Juries to follow trails that lead out of your jurisdiction. The criminal enterprises you are about to tackle have built themselves over generations, and are allied from sea to shining sea. Do not pick the fight until you are prepared to win it.

What you are doing is every bit as important as what our Founders did in the 1700s. They *designed* the machine to secure our liberty, but you are building and *running* it, for the first time in the history of the world.

Constitutional County Rollout Critical Path   2 23 JL

This is a way to look at, and to plan and measure your progress in, the Tactical Civics process for restoring our Republic through Rule of Law, on the ground in your own County or municipality.

Items with the same number may be done simultaneously or in any order. Items with higher numbers should not be attempted until all items with lower numbers have been completed.

I do not know your local conditions. Be prudent, ponder, consult, adapt!

1A *Formation of, or Contact with a presentable, willing, existing Militia group in the jurisdiction*
(For what such a group might look like, see American Militia 2.0: an American Militiaman's Handbook*)*

1B *Founding of a TC Chapter, or other Constitutionalist education-and-outreach group. Functions include recruiting additional members to help pack the governing-body meeting, general education, networking and outreach to and beyond the local the community, soliciting business support, and educating current and prospective Grand Juries*

1D *Contact with a rep from TC HQ to provide assistance. The TC organization may not want to deal with you if you are, or have partnered with, an existing militia group. In that case, contact John Leyzorek through securetheserights@protonmail.com*

2A *Build Militia group's capabilities, tactical, preparedness, response, intel, comms, and forensic.*

2B *Build Militia's comm, intel, and support networks in the region and beyond.*

2C *Build Tactical Civics awareness in community through Chapter activity or otherwise*

2D *Build awareness of and support for TC outside the Chapter such as business affiliates, relationships with service and fraternal organizations, teach about history, value, powers of Grand Jury, true nature and Constitutional mandate for Militia*

2E *Build Militia group's community recognition and reputation through service and outreach.*

3 *Develop outside support for Militia group, i.e. business affiliates, cooperative relationships with Sheriff or other paid LE, and community service groups and agencies.*

4A *Contact/recruitment with a member or members of the governing body willing to introduce and support the Grand Jury Ordinance, and Constitution Enforcement and Militia Ordinance. Meetings should probably be with individual members, to avoid both internal politics and potential Open Meetings Act violations.*

Do not be tempted to jump the gun and contact politicians early. It is important to wait until you have a large base of popular support and a highly capable militia group, i.e your movement is a force in its own right. The TC program of restoring control by the people and Rule-of Law is OPPOSED to the self-interest of politicians. You will get their support only if they are true, humble Constitutionalist public servants, OR if they see you as a political asset.

4B *Customize ordinances with proper names of jurisdiction and governing body, proper references to State law (work with TCHQ or John Leyzorek)*

4C *Be sure that your local Militia groups are clean, fully on-board, and ready for members to sign up; ready with command structure, standards, training protocol, by-laws, and officer list to report or submit for approval at County meeting.*

4D *Get Ordinances, Militia Signup, adoption of Regulations, and Appointment of Officers on the County governing body Agenda to make it all legal under Open Meetings Act.*

4E *Do not pick a fight you are not ready to win. WAIT until passage of the Ordinances is essentially certain before introducing them. Wait (and work!) if necessary to replace hostile local government members to assure passage. A defeat will damage the credibility and slow the progress of the movement far more than taking the time to engineer the right circumstances.*

5A *Turn out supporters for meeting, and pass ordinances!*

5B *Don't forget publicity. Success breeds success only if people* *know about it.*

6 *Existing and new Militia members sign up before the meeting ends, required procedures and other documents are submitted to governing body, officer lists are submitted and approved/appointed*

7A *TC Chapter or equivalent and Militia both continue community service and outreach*

7B *Militia continues and expands cooperation with paid LE and other community agencies*

7C *Milita and TC Chapter (or equivalent) develop and work with contacts in neighboring jurisdictions and adjacent States to duplicate their success over a larger area. A wide and strong network is essential BEFORE established criminal enterprises, in government or private sector, can be targeted.*

8A *Look for a criminal enterprise, such as drug-dealer, pimp, or corrupt contractor/public agency operation in your AO that is or can be made very unpopular, but has not been dealt with by paid LE. Compare its reach and power with the reach and power of your militia network. If your best judgement is that you are ready for it, petition for empanelment of a Grand Jury, and file presentments on your target to begin the process. Remember it is rule-of-law and its necessary due process that we are restoring and supporting..*

A private criminal enterprise is a better first target for your new Constitutional law-enforcement capability than an instance of government corruption or overreach, because we are still proving to the public the superior authority and effectiveness of We-the-People over the government apparatus. Of course it is never the true and legitimate government we must attack, but corrupt individuals who subvert or misuse its powers. But part of the resistance on the part of the criminal actors, will be to obscure that distinction. We need to build our reputation diligently and effectively, to counter that propaganda effort.

8B *TC Chapter or equivalent, assists with Grand Jury pool education and recruitment pursuant to Ordinance*

9 *Militia assists GJ with service of warrants, security, etc. Handling of processes and evidence must be faultless and exemplary.*

10A *Militia and Grand Jury support and closely monitor the prosecution and trial processes. Be alert to BOTH possible inappropriate dismissal or leniency suggesting the prosecutor or court is colluding with the criminal enterprise, AND violations of the accused's due-process rights. Reasonable suspicion of either must immediately trigger further investigation by Grand Jury with Militia support as needed.*

10B. *Publicity. TC Chapter/equivalent and Militia should use all their connections to assure wide and accurate publicity for the new era in Law Enforcement.*

11A *Rinse and repeat.*

11B *Continue to spread the movement, and build and strengthen networks, to enable successful targeting of more and more powerful and popular criminal actors. You must eventually reach the level of public confidence that will support you in taking down corrupt or oathbreaking State representatives, so as to de-criminalize your legislature. This is the goal not only for the mere sake of lawful government, but also to prepare it to complete ratification of the original First Article of Amendment ("Our First Right"/small districts, and the rest of the restoration process. (See TC Intro)*

APPENDIX E

Do You Want it the Hard Way?

We have been saying over and over, for years now, in slightly different forms, that our task to restore our Republic is *law enforcement*. Law enforcement. You know, what we grew up thinking was exclusively the cops' job, and no business of ours.

Has everyone noticed that all over our country, the law is in tatters? The cops continue getting to murders and robberies minutes or hours after they are over, and pulling us over for burned-out taillights, but our courts and our Congress seem to have forgotten that law exists at all? The Courts are running away from it, and Congress is making it up as they go along, with unbelievable arrogance and poker-faces, when they are not spraying spittle and palpable lies in pretend outrage, or crying crocodile tears?

I suppose everyone has also noticed another slightly terrifying development. We used to console ourselves after an election that went "the wrong way" by thinking, "Well, people will see how bad this is, and we can vote them out in two or four years". Can anyone seriously believe now, that the criminal globalists will let themselves be voted out in 2022 or 2024, after what they have just gotten away with?

We are in the midst of an historic catastrophe, as grave as Lincoln's War, if not worse. *Are we awake now?*

Our Republic has suffered a *coup d'etat,* but not one where an armed group imprisons or kills the rightful officers and takes their seats, while loyalists try to hold the line. In that sort of coup, you grab or kill the bad guys and the rightful government closes in behind, and heals. Alas today, nobody has the guts or the honesty to make the arrest, and there may be little or no legitimate government left to heal.

But we are patriots, and God's children, and despair must not be part of our vocabulary.

There are mountains of evidence of plain election fraud, in multiple States. If this is allowed to stand, the democratic process in our Republic is over, and its power will permanently be in the hands of people who utterly deny its legitimate purposes, and think of us as cattle at best, inconveniences to be erased at worst..   But it need not and it must not stand. So we are calling on you, our network.

So here is a way to think about turning this *catastrophe* into an *opportunity*, to begin turning the tide.

1. Do you live in any of the States where massive, provable election fraud took place last November?

2. Do you live in a County or a Township with a conservative or Constitution-supporting local government?

3. Do you have or can you build a large group of America-loving Constitutionalist friends in your County (perhaps as a Tactical Civics Chapter)?

4. Do you have a local Militia or community-watch or Second-Amendment or preparedness group in your County, a good one, an open, upright, public-spirited one? Or are you, or a friend of yours, willing to start one?

If you answered yes to all four questions, you can make history this year.The TACTICAL CIVICS™organization may, or www.securetheserights.net will, work with you step by step to get our program running on afterburners. There may be need need to polish the face and perfect the structure of that Militia group. It must have and work to keep the confidence and goodwill of the community and of local paid law enforcement.

You must build the numbers ofyour TACTICAL CIVICS™ chapter or equivalent group. It must hold meetings and lectures about how American government is supposed to work, and about how it has been twisted, and now *stolen.* Teach about the true powers and importance of the Grand Jury. You must build a group capable of turning out, let's just say, as big a crowd as has ever crammed itself into a meeting of your local government.

Hit up a member or (one at a time) members of local

government. Are they sad and frightened at what was done to our election? If you tell them, "It never has to happen again; in fact, the people who did it can be in jail before the next election rolls around", what will they say? If they ask, "How?", tell them about our plan for constitutional Law Enforcement, and show them the Ordinances that will make it possible, if they are passed.

If you've gotten this far, you are already most of the way through the process we describe in out County Handout, now in its 13th revision. You can find it here as Appendix D.

But now, let's go a bit farther. Let's war-game the battles that the Ordinances merely position us to fight.

We've been teaching that, once you have constitutional Militia by Ordinance, and you know or suspect criminal activity, you first petition (or demand; each state has a procedure) that a judge seat a Grand Jury. Once it is impaneled, you send it the evidence that you know of (it's called a presentment), and it investigates further. If paid law-enforcement is shy, too busy, or itslef under investigation, your Militia does the physical work of evidence collection, serving and seizing papers etc by subpoena and warrant. Eventually, an indictment is handed down, and if the accused is powerful maybe Militia has to make the arrest because it is too 'hot' for the paid guys. Book him, jail him, and the trial process then hopefully convicts him and sends him up the river.

But maybe it is not so smooth. Criminals in suits, with offices under granite domes, will pull a lot of strings to keep their rackets going.

What if the judge refuses to seat a Grand Jury? What if you go to the Sheriff, and he refuses, too? Lots of things, brothers and sisters!

First, repeat the petitions. Get your presentments (evidence of crime) to the news media....if the out-of-state owned papers will not run the story, put it on the radio, print up handbills and post them, get it out on blogs, set up a booth in front of your courthouse and hand out copies of your evidence that so-and-so the Big Shot is a criminal.

These are all protected exercises of Free Speech. If you think anyone will try to shut them down, remember you have constitutional Militia, recognized by the Constitution AND your local government to enforce the Law, which includes the First Amendment. Your Militia is also charged with suppressing insurrection, which means organized action against the legitimate government. Since the legitimacy of government rests on its service to the rights of We the People, any effort to suppress your political speech constitutes an insurrection, which your Militia is lawfully authorized and duty-bound to suppress.

Meanwhile, most states have a legal process for impeaching, removing or replacing a judge who misbehaves. Get it going!

Oh, yeah, you should be wondering, *why* does that judge not want a Grand Jury to look into what you suspect....Could it be (s)he is involved, or hoping to shield the criminal? Grounds for another presentment, this time against that judge for obstruction, conspiracy, etc. Follow the same process to demand a Grand Jury, publicize, and so on.

Does this all sound like a lot of work? What is America worth to us? How hard should we work to assure that we don't become West China?

Does the state supreme court (if that is how the process works in your state) refuse to remove the judge so you can have a Grand Jury? Well, well, co-conspirators everywhere! One of your guys should have a contact in the militia in your State capital. You know the process…

See the outline? Your Constitutionalist club and recognized constitutional Militia unit, with deep public support, raises an escalating, let us say, "manure-storm", around the system's refusal to do the obvious right thing and seat a Grand Jury.

You have yet *more* in your tool-box. Cartoons and ridicule were used to great effect in our American Revolution and many times after. Surely you have an artist and a jokesmith in your network. Sic them on the obstructors! Remember, *no* lawless physical threats! Ridicule, contempt, and describing how they're flouting the law and the will of the people.

Do not forget that your Militia is now recognized in your county as having the responsibility to *execute the law,* as set forth in the Constitution. Does that judge exceed the speed limit by one MPH on his way to work? Does he put out more trash than the city allows? Does he fail to sort his recyclables? Does he own rental property that he doesn't properly maintain? Does he seem to spend more money than his salary would support? And *all* the officials up the line who participate in the obstruction, get the same treatment, through cooperation with Militias and TC Chapters in the places where they live.

Do you remember Teddy Roosevelt's "Speak softly and carry a big stick?" And our buddy (or at least Biden's buddy) Chairman Mao, who said that power comes from the barrel of a gun?

All the while that you are putting overwhelming lawful, peaceful procedural pressure on anyone who obstructs your process of house-cleaning, your militia is conspicuously training with live ammo, according to its lawfully established and approved training schedule, perhaps in the field next to the Judge's favorite golf-course. Is that a hint? *Naaaah!*

There is no true trust or loyalty among criminals. Whoever is trying to block you *will* break; after all, you're just demanding that he *follow the Law* and sign a piece of paper!

You move on to the next step. If the jailer will not take in the man you arrest, same treatment. If the prosecutor will not bring the case that the Grand Jury hands down, same treatment. If the judge tries to dismiss, same treatment. The citizens just need to shake themselves out of our government-induced slumber; *We the People* are the highest level in the system of government that we instituted. And *they* are violating the law!

All the while, you're teaching and recruiting for TACTICAL CIVICS™ or similar clubs, and Militias, in neighboring counties.

We the People will not give up. We outnumber any force that can be sent against us. And the Law is not just on our side; it's *ours!*

APPENDIX F
An American Militiaman's Oath

I solemnly swear or affirm that to the best of my ability, I will do my duty to God, to my family, to my community and to the due processes of Law conformable to God's law, including properly constituted Grand Juries; that I will uphold the Constitutions of my State and of these United States, execute the Laws of that union, suppress Insurrections, and repel Invasions, giving aid and comfort to all in times of peril, and keeping myself physically, mentally, and morally fit. So help me, God.

APPENDIX G
A Sampling of Training Topics

1. Basic USAC, US Army Infantry Skills

    Offensive Patrolling Formations

Wedge	Security halts
Line	Patrol base
File	Crossing danger areas
Echelon	Ambush kill sacks
Vee	Diamond

2. Movement to Contact

    Actions at the objectives

    Rally points

    Line of departure

    Intel gathering

3. Defensive Position

       Perimeter, interlocking fires

       Early warning, booby trap, claymore

       Alternate location, fall back

       LP/OP

       Fighting positions

       Counter attack

4. Communications

       Dead letter Drop

       Civilian radios, Ham operators

       Land line

       Cell

       Discuss codes, secrets in sentence

       Discuss Fusion Center = Danger

5. Logistics – Food, Ammo, Med Supplies

       Vehicles

       Building materials

          Local

          Self

       How to cache food/med/weapon/ammo/clothing/commo

6. Medical – all trained at EMT level

       Underground Hospital

       Selected home hospital

       Herbs

Study of Botany

Movement of the injured

Aid and litter teams

Combat life saver

9. Vehicle Movements (heavy and light)

Formations

Movement to contact

Roadblocks

Intercept

Quick Ambush

React to Ambush

10. Home Defense

E&E

Survival Packs Contents

Spider Holes – hide, how, where

Barricades

Booby Traps – inside, outside

Escape early warning

Call for Assistance

11. Meetings

Who, what, when, where, why

everyone searched – phone, wire

Fusion center, other

12. Training – Scenario based

training lanes, CQB

Physical fitness

MMA – sentry stalking

Land Nav

Attack/Counterattack

Shooting skills, quick kill, all weapons

13. Martial Arts in depth

Michael Echanis knife

14. Secure Town avenues of approach

LP/OP How and Where

React Teams

Road Blocks

Ambush

Counterattack

15. Advanced Training

2,3,4 Man Kill Teams

Assassination > Selection

Body Snatches How To

IPB Intel Prep of battlefield

Body Disposal

Crime Scene Investigation

Combat Ops in Mountainous Terrain

Military Mountaineering

Recon/Surveillance

Demolition and Mines

Evasion/Survival

Troop Leading Procedure

Receive the Mission

Issue a warning order

Make tentative plan

Initiate movement

Re con   Complete plan

Issue complete order

Supervise, lead

Enemy

Composition

Disposition

Strength

Recent activities

Reinforcement capabilities

Possible COA's

Intel: SALUTE report

Size

Activity

Location

Unit

Time

Equipment

GET LOCATION IN CASE EVENT

16. Police Operations – how they operate

Police planning for takedown

Planned Checkpoints

No-Knock Raids

How they move into position

How they attack and occupy

How to exploit their strength and weakness

Commo: Theirs, Ours

Level of Training

17. Engineer

Sapper trained

Use local equipment

Obstacles

Trench warfare

vehicle traps

18. Air Assets

How they will be used

How to hide – very different

No large groups – movement – or in the defense

Drones – LP/OP

Appendix H Introduction to Tactical Civics™

(Please note that the author John Leyzorek no longer has any connection to the official Tactical Civics organization, and the following outline of the mission is his opinion only, and may not represent the official position of Tactical Civics™)

Our Republic, the United States of America, is unique in the history of the world, as the only organized society based on the principles that we belong to ourselves, because God made each of us, gave each of us life, and recognizes our individual right to make our own decisions and bear the consequences.

When we left the British Empire and built our own political structure, we built it on these facts, and on a deep knowledge of history and human nature. We created a watershed in history with our explicit statement, in our Declaration of Independence, that government's sole legitimizing purpose is to secure the rights of the governed. With our Constitution, we built ours, to protect the freedom God gave us.

That freedom, the system we built to defend it, and the prosperity it has allowed us to achieve, have been beacons to the whole world, for two centuries.

All this is threatened now, ultimately by our own laziness and cowardice. We are unfaithful to the principles our Founders cherished. We allow powerful interests to corrode our culture and steal our freedom. This struggle is as old as civilization, but we have been losing it, for a century and a half.

By the familiar combination of Divine Providence and hard work, a small group scattered around the country has developed a comprehensive plan, and begun a movement, to awaken us from, and teach us to repair, our dereliction. This is an engineered schedule of peaceful, lawful *actions* and reforms that will bring our government back under the control, and to the service, of We, the People who created it, and will go on to allow us to heal our civilization.

The plan and organization are called TACTICAL CIVICS™

Our first action must be to revitalize the only, and the essential, law-enforcement mechanisms specified in our Constitution but never yet deployed for the purpose. Article I Section 8 Clause 15 names the **Militia** as responsible for executing the laws of the Union, that is, the Constitution and all other law made in conformity to it. Militia is all of us. It must operate with recognition and regulation by, and coordination with government. But because Militia is We the People who ordained that government, it has the authority and duty to enforce the Law against officials and agencies, as much as against private individuals. The Constitution calls for specific support and coordination of Militia by the Congress and the States, but since both are in persistent violation of these duties, we provide an Ordinance, based on the Declaration's reversion principle, which commits local government to lawfully perform them. Militia must eventually replace all the vast unconstitutional, endemically corrupt and incessantly warmongering, terrorist alphabet agencies and military-industrial complex, but when first re-established it will be paid law-enforcement's best friend, as long as the paid guys stay within the Law.

Most important, violating the Constitution will no longer be a crime that every official gets away with.

Directing Militia in this task, the **Grand Jury** is an institution a thousand years old, which we inherit from English Common Law. Corrupt judges and prosecutors have made it a lap-dog, but we will educate the people to know their essentially unlimited power to investigate crime, once seated as Grand Jurors, supporting the process through another Ordinance.

 Revitalized Militia (all of us and our neighbors) will be able to arrest criminals however powerful, upon indictment by the Grand Jury, and force their lawful trial. *No more* will corrupt officials and agencies protect each other, as they ignore and pervert the Law, and eat out our substance.

Beginning our reformation at the local level is essential, because not only our federal government apparatus but our states are too deeply corrupted to be brought back under the Law by any amount of mere persuasion. And freedom, like tyranny, is local. We can make the vicious ambitions of the gobalists irrelevant in our own communities, NOW.

But once We the People reclaim the Law as Grand Juries and the sword as Militia in enough communities, and a critical mass of other citizens see the functioning value of applied, correct American civics, the State legislatures will be ready to cooperate in Tactical Civics(TM)'s next effort.

It is called **Our First Right**.™ It seeks to complete ratification by the States, of the original First Article in the Bill of Rights, which guarantees Congressional Districts of less than 50,000 people. This will bring real representation to most of the country, which now effectively belongs only to the culturally bankrupt big cities. This, on top of Constitutional law-enforcement, will purge Congress of career parasites, and encourage ordinary decent people to run, be elected, and give us true self-government, rather than rule by paid lackeys of industry and of the globalists. Small districts will lower the cost of a campaign to an affordable level with no room for dirty money.

Fourth stage: One Congressman for each 50,000 citizens adds up to over 6,400, which will not fit in the Capitol building in D.C . Most of our new Representatives will have run on a promise to pass our **Bring Congress Home Act™,** which will create the world's first distributed legislature: Congress will meet by Internet, each Representative and Senator from his or her own sole, small office in their own district, under the watchful eye of the People whom they represent, not in DC wining and dining with the lobbyists. Honest men and women will no longer have to abandon their families and businesses and work in the cesspool of D.C., to serve us for limited terms in Congress.

Complementing functioning Grand Juries and Militia, working to *keep* straight our decriminalized Congress is our **Indictment Engine™**. This mechanism, possibly run as an artificial-intelligence app, will test every proposed law in the country against the Constitution and the laws of the State in which its sponsors reside. If a proposed "law", or other government action, violates the law, the Grand Jury in the appropriate jurisdiction will be informed, and the violator will withdraw it, or face prosecution.

Beyond these five major actions, TC has a laundry-list of further reforms for the new, truly representative Congress to pass, to end the theft-by-counterfeiting of our money, to sunset lawless agencies, to end our global bullying and our subsidy of tyrants, to protect our borders, and more.

All the details, and a large library of legal and historical references, can be found through the organization, www.tacticalcivics.com, or through the person who sent you this outline. This is not pie-in-the-sky. This is not revolution. This is merely enforcement of the magnificent system of law that our forefathers were inspired to create for themselves and their posterity.

No mass-movement or leader can rescue our civilization. But YOU can start this sea-change, YOU can put your finger in the dike that protects most of what we hold dear, by founding your own Tactical Civics Chapter in your own County, and pursuing legal recognition of your militia group..

Go to www.tacticalcivics.com, or e-mail securetheserights@protonmail.com, to begin.
John Leyzorek February 2023

End Note

Much of the urgency we see in the project this book discusses, comes from the perspective that we are in a crisis. The satanic criminal globalist cabals threaten everything that is good. They threaten not only our political freedom, our security in possessions, our health, our children, our worship, even our lives, but they threaten the concept and heritage of the moral agent under God, the concept that has lifted millions out of slavery and remains a lamp of hope for billions.

I have said that the subject of this book is only a part of the larger plan that can preserve and spread that fire. It is a big plan, a big task, a work for our lifetimes and more. I am feeling tired already!

I belong to a tiny community-preparedness group here in the mountains, trying to serve the community, learning to help each other, and puzzling about how to till and amend our soil so we can some day grow that *necessary* militia. After every global-doom-and-gloom bull-session, we say, "How does that affect what we do tomorrow?"

And the answer is, essentially not at all. We still need to manage such supply inventory as we can afford, still need to poke wood into the stove (and probably cut more), still keep looking for needs in the community we must fill, still keep eyes and ears open for another person who is looking be a part of the solution ('though they may not know it). It is February as I write. Garden cleaning, planning and prepping is part of each mild day. It is all part of the Great Plan, but each item is necessary in itself, and valuable in itself.

If we get all the way to bringing Congress home, before God turns out the lights, to have been a part of restoring the kind of Republic our founders imagined will have been an amazing acomplishment.

If we do not get that far, but do decriminalize our State capitals, that by itself will be worth doing.

If only ours and two other Counties get our Ordinances passed and we put away the kidnapping ring, we can feel deep gratitude for the opportunity to have been a part of that.

If our militia and County Constitutionalists Club merely force the crooks out of County government and replace them with decent people by diligent door-knocking at election time, that will be a service to God and our fellow men.

If one or two wild teenagers just learn to be upright men and women (and a lot about guns) by participating in our training and rubbing shoulders with responsible adults, their children will thank us and there will be rejoicing in Heaven.

If all we accomplish is to meet a few neighbors we can trust, is that not by itself a blessing?

I do not want you the reader to put this book down feeling overwhelmed by the magnitude of the task before us, OR complacent that doing only what is easy, is enough. But understand the each of the myriad small steps is in itself a blessing, and a mitzvah. So has the opportunity to write this book been, for me.

About the Author

John Leyzorek, father, teacher, engineer, farmer, and freedom-fighter, was born in 1956 in Ohio. His father, a pioneer in business computing applications, taught him to use and value tools, that there was nothing he could not learn how to do, and to identify poison ivy. John learned to love the natural world lurking in the invisible wilderness of central New Jersey.

He cut his engineering teeth doing a mix of defense- and renewable-energy-related research in a university environment in the early 1980s. During this time he started his own business providing at one end consulting services for university and industrial clients, and at the other, economical repair services for local farmers and industries.

He migrated to a mountain farm in West Virginia at the end of the 1980s, seeking to realize his dream of what manufacturing engineers call "vertical integration" and preppers call self-sufficiency, not only for its survival value, but as a place in which to teach his children where everything comes from, how to see the Law and Providence of God in all things, and to connect emotionally to the whole of human history.

Trying to engineer a righteous and frugal way of life and find a place in a new community, John came up hard against the difference between the beautiful and Godly conceptions in our Declaration of Independence and Constitution, and the sordid reality of the modern administrative state. He learned about what is and is not Law, studying, arguing, and litigating several issues *pro se* all the way to the Supreme Court of West Virginia, and acquired a deep commitment to the Founders' dream of a constitutionally limited Republic serving responsible citizens.

Seeking to live these duties brought him to the mission of TACTICAL CIVICS™, and to a world of brothers he had never met: the Militia.